# 1881–1968

*photograph by L. Stuart*

# Conor
## 1881–1968

*The life and work
of an Ulster artist
by*
Judith C. Wilson

*With a critical appreciation
by*
*John Hewitt*

*and*

*Foreword
by*
Kenneth Jamison

Blackstaff Press

*To
my parents
with gratitude
for their
encouragement and support*

Published by Blackstaff Press, 3 Galway Park, Dundonald, BT16 0AN, with the assistance of the Arts Council of Northern Ireland

ISBN 0 85640 230 3

Filmset and printed in Great Britain by BAS Printers Limited, Over Wallop, Hampshire

*Cover: The Launch* by William Conor
*Back cover and frontispiece:* William Conor

# CONTENTS

# LIST OF ILLUSTRATIONS

# FOREWORD

I have an early recollection of my mother pointing from the top of a tramcar to a small figure in an ample overcoat, black bow and a soft hat that had long become comfortable to the contours of its wearer. I was later to see the silk handkerchief that issued from the breast pocket. The cumulative effect was faintly flamboyant rather than fashionable, for the trousers showed no vestige of a crease and the hat was old. The bow, its rival in age, was imprecisely tied, its loose ends cascading with just a hint of cultivated carelessness. But the mild indulgence of this habitual dress was enough to assert his calling. 'That is Mr. Conor, the artist,' my mother said. As I looked, the tram rattled out of the Stranmillis Road leaving behind the rusticated facade of the Belfast Museum and Art Gallery.

I have another memory of that building from about the same time. On Saturday mornings for several years we pressed into the lecture theatre, eager for the flickering screen. These film showings were prefaced by ritual. First the clouds of institutional disinfectant calculated to combat any contagion. After the spraying, a familiar, bespectacled figure was cheered the length of the lecture hall to the stage where, from a lectern at the side, he announced the programme. 'The Museum Man' we called him, and I can still hear the distinctive intonation of his voice. Then the lights dimmed, more applause, the projector whirred.

If William Conor was our artist, John Hewitt seemed the embodiment of our Museum. It was some years before I was to place his influence more precisely in the art galleries where his presence, whether he was there or not, would often be implied by the lingering aroma from his companionable briar.

It was not until 1957 that I actually met William Conor and, when I did, it was in John Hewitt's flat on a wet December night on a melancholy occasion. John and his wife Roberta, both of whom I had come to know well, gave a farewell party before leaving for Coventry where John had been appointed the first Art Director of the new Herbert Art Gallery and Museum. I was to succeed him as art correspondent of the *Belfast Telegraph*, which I did with considerable misgiving for he had established the art column with authority and literary distinction. There seemed a certain bleak finality in the four articles he contributed on his departure to the *Telegraph*'s 'Saturday Miscellany' and in which he set out his recollections of some of the artists he had known over the years. When he and Roberta returned to Belfast in 1972, a number of those who had gathered for that farewell party were gone, William Conor among them.

My own spell as art critic for the *Telegraph* came to an end in 1962 when I joined the staff of CEMA, which later became the Arts Council. My office was not far from the Linen Hall Library where Willie Conor was at home with the gentle librarian, Jimmy Vitty. From there I could expect him, for a time, once or twice a week. We would retire to a snug in Charlie Lavery's in May Street for soup and stew and one or two glasses of whiskey. These congenial surroundings were right for reminiscence. As with most old men, his narrative was furnished at each rehearsal with the same phrases and gestures. Little emerged of firm chronology. But these anecdotes were interesting for the light they shed on the artist's personality. In each he featured in an almost Chaplinesque way, always the fall-guy, the loser, invariably the odd man out. In later years these stories of youthful shyness became part of the mythology, like the mild eccentricities of dress. The dignity of the man was a compound of genuine humility, of a strong inner reserve and of an awareness of his destiny as an artist in the city of his birth, a city unaccustomed to artists.

I do not imagine that these well-attested anecdotes, available to her from the recollections of Conor's friends or from tapes of the artist reminiscing in old age, will have been of much help to Judith Wilson who has undertaken the formidable task of writing the artist's 'life'. Indeed, had she taken on a similar challenge for some artist of an earlier time and another place, she might well have found her task easier. Documentary evidence on Conor is scarce – a handful of letters in the Linen Hall Library, a few dates fixed firmly in the framework of external reference and the records provided by exhibition catalogues. All have been searched and collated and to the few secure dates Judith Wilson has striven painstakingly to relate the frail testimony of reminiscence. That she has produced so readable and so coherent an account is a tribute to her diligent scholarship. Whatever can be verified is set out in her patient text.

Conor's death in 1968 was felt throughout the city. Townsend Street Presbyterian Church could scarcely contain those who assembled in its austere aisles to pay their last respects – fellow artists, actors, writers, representatives of civic and political life, friends. That quiet, reserved, gentle man, as in an allegory, had conquered his native city by steadfastness and charity.

John Hewitt returned to Belfast in 1972, his professional career honourably accomplished, his reputation as a poet secure and his creative impulse undiminished. He has devoted much of his retirement to reflecting on events in which he himself played no small part. The sturdy vignettes that appeared in the *Telegraph*'s 'Saturday Miscellany' have been expanded and set in context in his comprehensive survey of Art in Ulster up to 1957. He has written monographs on his friends John Luke and Colin Middleton – and now we have this perceptive critical analysis of the work of William Conor. It is characteristic of him that this publication is in collaboration with a much younger author, for John Hewitt has never failed to extend a curatorial care for those who follow as for those who have gone before.

KENNETH JAMISON
Director, Arts Council of Northern Ireland

# ACKNOWLEDGEMENTS

My first and greatest debt is to Mrs Richard Hayward, who not only led me to the art of William Conor by suggesting this research, but whose invaluable and generous work throughout has been the major contribution to the making of this book. I wish also to record my thanks to her for permission to quote from the writings of Richard Hayward.

My particular appreciation is due also to Mr William Carter for thoughtful reminiscences of the artist; they have the quality of sincere family friendship, while imparting a deeper knowledge of Conor the man.

To Mrs Mercy MacCann, better known as Mercy Hunter, and to Mr. Herbert Bell I am also indebted for information about William Conor that derived from their friendship with him, and for having been permitted to listen to tape recordings of their own conversations with the artist.

Mr Rowel Friers spoke freely with me about Conor, and of the artistic techniques which Conor had learned at David Allen and Sons, which were to influence him all his life. He also remembered some of the sadder aspects of the artist's last years.

I owe special thanks to Mr Michael Williams for several useful and informative conversations and for his permission to quote from letters written by his father, R. V. Williams (Richard Rowley) which are amongst the Conor Papers and the Lynn Doyle Papers. He also allowed me to include an extract from the Appreciation by Richard Rowley in *The Irish Scene*.

It gives me pleasure also to thank Mr Padraic Woods for having contributed memories of his fellow artist and friend.

To Mr James Vitty, former Librarian of the Linen Hall Library, Belfast, kinsman to the artist and an Executor of his Will, I wish to express my gratitude for having granted me free and full access to the private papers.

My thanks are also due to these relatives of William Conor who kindly provided me with various items of information about the artist's family: Mr E. M. Connor, Mr W. A. Connor (nephews), Mrs J. H. Brown and Mrs R. G. Kelly and their parents, the late Mr Matthew Milliken (cousin) and Mrs Milliken.

I also wish to thank Aberdeen University Library, Scotland, the American Consulate General, Northern Ireland, Mr W. A. Hoy; the American Irish Historical Society, New York, The Vicar General, Archdiocese of New York, Rt Rev Msgr Joseph T. O'Keefe; Armagh County Museum, Mr D. R. M. Weatherup, Curator; Army Head-quarters Northern Ireland, the Arts Council of Northern Ireland, Atkinson Art Gallery, Southport, England, the Barbican Gallery, Plymouth, England; B. T. Batsford Ltd., London, (for permission to reproduce a passage from *The Spirit of Ireland* by Lynn Doyle); Belfast Education and Library Board, Central Library, Mr Ivor Crawley, Chief

Librarian, for permission to quote letters from the Lynn Doyle Papers; the Belfast Telegraph Newspapers Ltd., The Bell Gallery, Belfast, Mr Nelson Bell; Mrs F. E. Benner, Mr and Mrs James Black, Bray Urban District Council Public Library, Republic of Ireland; British Broadcasting Corporation, Northern Ireland, Mr J. B. Hawthorn, B.B.C. Controller N.I.; The Brooklyn Museum, New York; Mrs A. C. Brooke; the *Bulletin*, Philadelphia; Lady Mairi Bury, Mr and Mrs Wilfred M. Capper, Mrs R. Clarke, Dr R. S. J. Clarke, Mr Douglas Carson, Mr Mike Catto; Central Office of Information, London, the Central Reference Library, Swansea, Wales; Century Newspapers, Ltd., (*News Letter*, Belfast); The Chelsea Arts Club, London; Church House, Armagh, Mr W. J. Dickson, Diocean Secretary; City Art Gallery, Manchester, Mr Timothy Clifford, Director; City Museum and Art Gallery, Plymouth, England, The Copley Plaza, Boston, U.S.A; Warren K. Cook Ltd., Toronto, Mr W. A. Cook, President; Mr W. J. Coombes, Mr and Mrs J. Cornett, Rev Robert R. Cox, Miss M. W. Cunningham; *The Daily Express*, London; Lord Horder for Gerald Duckworth & Co. Ltd., (for permission to reproduce letters from this firm to William Conor); Mr C. F. D. Dunbar, The Most Hon. The Marquess of Dufferin and Ava, Mrs A. Fowweather; Galway County Council Public Library; Mr Dan Gilbert; Glasgow Art Gallery, Grand Lodge of A.F. & A. Masons of Ireland, Dublin; Miss Norah Haughton, Mr Wilfred J. Haughton, Mrs J. A. Henshall, the late Miss M. Hirsch, Dr H. Montgomery Hyde; the Imperial War Museum, London; Mrs Denis Ireland; the *Irish News*, Belfast, the *Irish Times*, Dublin, the *Irish Press*, Dublin; Mr R. B. Jackson, the late Mr L. A. Kaitcer; Messrs Kennedy and Wolfenden, Belfast; Mrs Harry Cooke Knox and the late Mr Harry Cooke Knox, the Kraushaar Gallery, New York; Miss M. Y. Lawrence; Leeds City Art Gallery; Mrs A. Lewinter-Frankl; The Linen Hall Library, Belfast; The Most Hon. The Marquess of Londonderry, Mr and Mrs George McClelland, Mr Reggie McClure, Mrs J. D. McCord, Mr Richard MacCullagh, Miss J. P. McDowell, Mrs R. McRandal, Mr W. Grenville Mackie; James Mackie & Sons Ltd., for permission to include their photographic reproduction of Conor's drawing 'Munition Workers at Mackies'; Miss M. L. Magill; Malone Gallery, Ltd., Mr Howard Ruderman; Mr H. E. O. Mayne; The Metropolitan Museum of Art, New York; The Mitchel Library, Glasgow; Museum of Fine Arts, Boston; Municipal Gallery of Modern Art, Dublin; The National Library, Dublin; The National Library of Wales; the Clerk to the Northern Ireland Assembly, Stormont; Oakland Antiques, Belfast, the Oriel Gallery, Dublin, The Palace Bar, Dublin, Phaidon Press Ltd., Oxford, (for permission to quote an extract from *The Cubist Epoch* by Douglas Cooper); the *Philadelphia Inquirer*; Princess Gardens School, Belfast, Board of Governors; Public Records Office, Belfast; Dr and Mrs G. B. Purse; The Queen's University of Belfast; Raceview Woollen Mills, Ltd., Mr Michael Shepherd, Managing Director; Miss D. M. P. Ritchie; the Royal Academy of Arts, London; the Royal Glasgow Institute of the Fine Arts; the Royal Hibernian Academy of Arts, Dublin; the Royal School Armagh, Mr T. W. Mulryne, Headmaster; the Royal Society of Portrait Painters, London; The Rt Rev Msgr Arthur Canon Ryan, for permission to quote from the tribute to William Conor by Dr James Ryan; Mr John J. Sheill; Mrs M. P. Smiles; the Spook Farm Gallery, New Jersey; the *Sunday Press*, Dublin; Trinity College Library, Dublin; Ulster Carpet Mills Ltd., Mr W. O. Wilson, Director; Ulster Folk and Transport Museum, Mr G. B. Thompson, Director; Ulster Museum and Art Gallery, Dr W. A. McCutcheon, Director; Ulster Polytechnic, Art and Design Centre, Belfast; Ulster Television Ltd., Mr R. B. Henderson, Managing Director; United States of America, Department of the Army, Historical Services Division, Washington, D.C.; University College Dublin; Victoria and Albert Museum (Library), London; Victoria College, Belfast, Board of Governors; Vose Galleries, Boston; The Walker Art Gallery, Liverpool; Mr James A. Warwick; West Glamorgan County Library, Wales; The Whitworth Art Gallery, Manchester; Mr Kenneth W. Withers.

Thanks are due to the photographic departments of the Arts Council of Northern Ireland, The Brooklyn Museum, New York, The City Art Gallery, Manchester, The Ulster Folk and Transport Museum, The Ulster Museum, Belfast; also to Mr Dermott Dunbar, James Mackie and Sons Ltd, and particularly to the commissioned photographer Mr Ivan Strahan.

J.C.W.

# 1

# STREET SHADOWS
# AND
# SUNLIGHT

William Conor was born in 1881 and he died in 1968; within this span of years was lived the life of a man who followed his own feelings and was true to himself, a shy and humble man who, aware of the differences in the economic and social levels in the community, was able to bridge any such barriers by a humour which was kind but shrewd. His honesty in realising that he could only do his best if he accepted the terms of his own existence and its limitations and of his being one with his own working people, enabled him to see them through eyes of love and understanding and to devote his art to the recording of ways of life which have now largely disappeared.

He was a warm and genuine person. I have noticed time and time again when interviewing people who had known Conor that they would pause for a moment and then would smile or perhaps laugh with affection as an amusing incident came to mind. Always they would speak first of his being very lovable, of his gentleness, or of a quality of innocence which never left him. These comments confirm the impressions I have received from his pictures and have strengthened the identity of artist and man. The faces in his pictures reflect these qualities with delight, anticipation and dignity, whatever may be the backgrounds of the subjects, but most outstanding is the impression of innocence. Children with impish smiles, making you believe they are plotting their next move, are portrayed without malice but with childish fun. His stark war sketches, his scenes of domestic poverty are never without heart. Compassion is implied and it seems to me that a viewer can only experience the pictures in full if this is accepted. Conor for me has the merit of portraying folk without being 'folksy'.

1. *Courtin'*.
Pur. 1922. Oil on canvas.
75.6 × 50.2 cms
Ulster Museum Collection,
Belfast.

William Conor was the fourth in a large Presbyterian family of seven children, Matthew, Hugh, Mary, William, John, Russell and Martin. He was born on 9 May 1881, at 5 Fortingale Street, off the Old Lodge Road, Belfast. His father, William Connor, who married Mary Wallace, was a tinsmith and sheet metal worker who later became a gasfitter. Although according to Conor he was 'a bit too fond of the bottle' he produced creative articles in copper and silver and 'left some lovely things behind'. Conor felt that any artistic abilities which he had were inherited through his father but that there was more intelligence on his mother's side.

He began his education on 19 March 1888, at the age of six at Clifton Park Central National School in Avoca Street, off Cliftonpark Avenue, Belfast, known locally as Erskine's school after the founder and principal, Alexander Erskine. It was here that he had lessons in reading, spelling, writing, arithmetic, grammar, geography, music and drawing although it was not until 1891 that he sat his first drawing examination. He did not regard himself as being able to draw well, even though he said his drawings were very often displayed as an example to the other children.

At a time when every boy has some thoughts about his future, when parents try to decide what is best for their child, the future of a boy such as William Conor is often helped by the chance of his being in the right place at the right time.

On one occasion he accompanied a school friend to his music lesson at the office of Louis Mantell, Commissioner for taking Affidavits to USA Consul, at 5 May Street, Belfast. Louis Mantell was also the 'excellent precentor' in Fisherwick Presbyterian Church and had 'a charming light tenor voice'. The young William, being left to roam around, found the temptation of a large bare wall so great that he began to cover it with chalk drawings. At the end of the music lesson Louis Mantell came out from his room and saw the drawings. Instead of being angry, he recognised Conor's talent and praised him. Later Mantell contacted his neighbour George Trobridge, who lived at 2 Mountpleasant, Stranmillis, and was an Associate of the Royal College of Art, London, and Headmaster of the Belfast Government School of Art. This resulted in Trobridge writing to Conor's parents suggesting that their son should go to the School of Art and take up drawing in a professional manner and that he would look after him.

So William Conor began his art education at the Belfast Government School of Art in 1894 at the age of thirteen. The School, situated in College Square North adjacent to the Royal Belfast Academical Institution, was at that time an extensive building consisting of four large rooms and a sculpture gallery, though it was reported in the Belfast Street Directory of 1897, that the School was not 'in as flourishing a condition as it should be, but efforts are now being made to improve this state of affairs'. At that time the School was given over to the teaching of Damask and Embroidery Design, although Conor himself said that his studies there began with Freehand and finished with Life Drawing.

At this School he was to meet a number of students who were to become well known locally if not internationally, such as the eight

2. Kettle and Stand made by Conor's father from copper and brass.
Private collection.

2

Morrow brothers, five of whom became illustrators (perhaps the best known being George who was connected with *Punch* from 1906, becoming art editor for five years in 1932); Charles Braithwaite (who was awarded a scholarship to the Royal College of Art, London, and was on the staff of the Methodist College, Belfast from 1909 until his death in 1941); W. R. Gordon (banner painter and landscape artist), who in 1896 was appointed to be one of the Pupil Teachers. Paul Henry particularly impressed Conor with his bohemian dress of black sombrero and long hair reaching to his shoulders, large black bow, velvet jacket and peg top trousers. Perhaps it was due to Henry's influence that Conor himself began to wear a bow tie, which as the years went on more closely resembled the artist's traditional bow. Rowel Friers describes it as being 'of the heavy knitted silk which worked its way loose at one side so that it never sat plumb'. And 'his wee black hat with a brim so buckled you would have thought he had boiled it before putting it on' was to be associated with his appearance all his life, as was 'his rather bow-legged walk', so described by John Hewitt.

As a step towards improving conditions, the School Board and the Council of the County Borough agreed that the building should be taken over by the Corporation as their headquarters and that the Government School of Art should cease to exist, 'pending the erection of the Municipal Technical Institution in College Square, the foundation stone of which was laid by His Excellency the Lord Lieutenant of Ireland (Earl of Dudley) upon the 24th of November, 1902'.

Although George Trobridge, whom Conor had regarded as 'the man behind me', lost his position as Headmaster when the School was taken over, Conor was to spend a further two years (1902–04) at the renamed school. Conor was now under the tuition of the Head Art Master, R. A. Dawson, for whom he did not have a high regard – 'Dawson didn't like me and I didn't like Dawson'. He also entered Alfred Baker's Life Class, but before doing so he received sound training in the Antique (a study of plaster cast classical figures and architectural models) for which he felt there was a 'snobbish worship' although by 1903 he had made such progress as to become Assistant Teacher in Antique.

During these years he passed a number of examinations. In 1895 he had obtained first place in Freehand and in Light and Shade. In the following year, with others, he had a First Class pass in Elementary Art Examinations, first place in Model Drawing in 1898, in Antique in 1901, in Anatomy and Life Drawing in 1903 and in that same year he achieved second place in the painting of Ornament and of Still Life; in local competition first place for a Head from Life, and for Studies in Hands and Feet, and second place in Draped Study. His performance in these examinations showed he had the competence to make studies of objects and in anatomy which were technically accurate yet in later years his sketches of people, while always conveying human feeling, were not always anatomically correct.

He left the Technical Institute in 1904 and later said that he found the teaching of that period to be 'a mechanical soulless drudgery'. Once again chance or fate changed his course of direction; in June of that year he had completed an application form to attend a short course on figure composition at the South Kensington and British Museums, London. Unfortunately his form arrived too late for consideration. He became apprenticed to David Allen and Sons, Belfast, a firm of Lithographers, where he worked in the poster design department at a wage of 4s 6d a week.

As a lithographer he had to make posters; at that time, most of these were hand drawn. The lithographer's 'tool' was a slab of limestone upon which he drew with a black wax crayon. Those who, like Conor, used the black crayon were known as the 'Blackmen'; they would reproduce separately in black each area of colour from the sketch in front of them. This had to be accurate, as did their knowledge of how much colour pigment was needed for each black area so that the printer, after adding special treatment to the block which allowed many copies to be made, could produce a print identical to the original sketch. Conor came to love the feeling of drawing with the smooth, waxy crayon on the textured stone surface and, after leaving David Allen and Sons, he continued to use wax crayons in his own work. He also discovered that rough paper felt much the same as the stone and that its use allowed him to achieve the same bold effect. In many of his pictures one can see his use of scuffling, a method in which he would scrape away with a sharp blade parts of his wax crayon drawing to intensify the highlights and

3. The Artists' Room, David Allen & Sons.
L–r; Gerry Burns, Conor, Billy Bell, Harry Graham, and Billy Corr.
Photograph from the Conor papers.

give a granular texture. He also discovered that a softer effect could be achieved by ironing the reverse sides of his crayon drawings. Unfortunately, as those were often done on flimsy paper some of the works were damaged by suffering singe or even burn marks. His use of mono printing also stemmed from the time spent at David Allen's. He would create an image, take a print from it and then work on the print. That is one reason why there is often a strong similarity between one picture and another.

An interesting and amusing description of William Conor and friends during their time spent together at David Allen's is given by Florence Mary McDowell in her book *Roses and Rainbows*. Florence Mary McDowell's brother Len, boarding in Bloomfield, Belfast,

> . . . speedily made friends with three young brothers who lived nearby. They were Herbie, Billy and Charlie Corr, gifted commercial artists at David Allen's. They introduced Len to their work-mate and bosom friend, Willie Connor, while Len in his turn introduced them all to his friend, Stanley Wilson.

Stanley Wilson, a member of the family who owned the Doagh Flax Spinning Mill, was the proud possessor of a motor cycle and side car and

> . . . it was soon the custom for all six young men to get somehow into or on to Stanley's motor-bike and take off for the week-end to Bridge House . . .

4. Conor and friends at the cottage in Craigavad.
L–r; Gerry Arneill, Herbie Corr, Conor, Pinkerton and Gerry Burns.
Photograph from the Conor papers.

After having been greeted by Aunt Laetitia, at Bridge House, Doagh, and fed, family and friends

... retired to the drawing-room and the old piano there. Almost everyone could both play and sing. Only Mary had to sit idly by and admire with shining eyes, with Willie Connor (about to drop an 'n' and become Conor, the first step on his way to being the eventual doyen of Irish painters), who was worse-off than Mary even, being tone-deaf. He, too, was desperately ambitious to be musical, and with the help of his friends and the family, did learn by rote one tune on the keyboard – 'The West's Awake'. That splendid black head, that fine profile, those dark brilliant eyes of Conor, all glowed and shone with an ambition realised, as his strong sensitive right hand struck out a mal-fingered melody line of passionate sentiment while his equally strong sensitive left hand, not knowing what the right was doing, maintained a steady thump, thump, thump on the C below middle C. His happiness was complete. His ambition realised. He never learnt another tune, but sat back happily sketching his friends round the piano, where, immortalised by him, they remained for ever on paper, to be hung for evermore over Mary's mantelpiece.

When they were not at Bridge House they would all go

... to their seventh heaven, a little labourer's cottage at Craigavad. They all clubbed together with two more artists, Gerry Burns and Gerry Arneill from Allen's, to pay the infinitesimal rent and to buy food. Here they did as they pleased, from Saturday lunch until very early Monday breakfast. They slept, basked in the sun, drank beer, painted, drew, talked, sang, talked, played and talked.

5. *Three views of a horse and rider*.
11 February 1910. Pencil on paper.
13.9 × 21 cms
Linen Hall Library Collection, Belfast.

# 2

# ... AND THE
# FIRST BRIEF
# JOURNEYS

Conor was now developing a spontaneous drawing technique by recording quick impressions and it soon became a habit for him to put on a cloth cap and shabby clothes and go out into the streets with a newspaper, which contained loose leaves from his sketch book. When he saw anything of interest he leant against a lamp post or a wall, took out his newspaper as though he were simply reading the sports results and sketched away. Having to work so rapidly to set down on paper what he saw, he unconsciously achieved a personal style.

William Carter recalls that Conor told him of his frequent visits to Johnson's Horse Repository at University Road, Belfast, where he was able to make many study sketches of the horses there. These were to be of great value to him in depicting horse races, hunts and fairs.

During 1906 the Connor family went to live at 3 Landscape Terrace, their fifth change of house since Conor's birth. By 1884 they had left 5 Fortingale Street, due to redevelopment, to go to number 6 across the road. Three years later they were living at 22 Fortingale Street; by 1890 they occupied 51 Glenfarne Street which became number 45 when the street was renumbered during 1892. After living there for twelve years they removed to 40 Perth Street for four years from 1902 until 1906. Conor was now twenty-five years old.

The turn of the century saw the beginning of a Gaelic revival in the literary and art worlds and possibly this influenced William Conor between 1907 and 1909 to use the Gaelic form of his name, signing either as 'Liam', 'Liam Conor' or, very occasionally, 'Liam O'Concohair'.

6. A sketch Conor made of his friend Gerry Burns.
7 October 1908. Pencil on paper.
21 × 13 cms
Linen Hall Library Collection, Belfast.

These changes were for a short period and I have seen them only on a few of his sketching notes.

There is no record of the actual date when Conor left David Allen's but it was possibly around 1910. In that year he first appeared on the membership list – and as an exhibiting member – of the Belfast Art Society. The five works hung were *Reflections*; *Evening – Dufferin Dock, Or Fantastic Bridge Athwart a Flood of Crystal*; *Dredger, Milewater Basin*; and *Unloading Coal, Albert Quay*.

Although Conor had become skilled in a trade, he knew he did not want to spend his life working in a lithographic firm.

> I was ambitious and wasn't interested in the future of that life; I wanted to be something better and I was drawing, drawing, drawing. I also thought that I should be interesting myself in physiognomy. Physiognomy deals with the character of one's features. I started to study this very much. I went to the Library in Royal Avenue and got out books on physiognomy.

Amongst his early sketches I found quite a number of head studies, especially of women.

It was Mrs Fowweather, daughter of Florence Mary McDowell, who told me that when he left David Allen's Conor lived for a short time at the cottage in Craigavad and then went to stay for some months on the Blasket Islands in Dingle Bay, Co Kerry – probably on the Great Blasket as this was the only one inhabited. James Vitty, a kinsman of Conor's, remembers hearing him speak of his not having much money and living in one of the Islanders' cottages. This would have suited Conor well, as on the island 'the living was rough but good'. While he was there he must surely have met Thomás Ó Crohan and Peig Sayers, two characters whose memories of island life were later translated from the Irish – *The Islandman*, first published in 1929 and *An Old Woman's Reflections*, published in 1962.

A number of artists and writers at this time went to the islands of Ireland where the traditional ways of life and the early Gaelic speech were still to be found. W. B. Yeats and John Millington Synge knew the Aran Islands and Synge visited the Blaskets in 1905, four years before his death.

Echlin Neill, landscape artist and friend of Conor, has recalled that Conor's workmate Gerry Burns was also an amateur violinist who played at night in the orchestra of the Grand Opera House, Belfast. Although there is no confirmation that Conor accompanied him to the theatre, he perhaps saw several of Synge's plays when they were performed in Belfast; among those were *Riders to the Sea* at the Theatre Royal in 1908 and *The Playboy of the Western World* at the Grand Opera House in 1909. We do know, however, that Conor was interested in the theatre and made several sketches of artistes who appeared in reviews. One of these, a pen and ink drawing *At the Empire 1910*, may be seen at the Ulster Folk and Transport Museum.

It seems that Conor lived for a short time in Dublin and years later, while being driven into Dublin by his friend William Carter, he had pointed out the district where he had stayed. He also visited County Donegal, making sketches there; pictures of Kinlough and Ardara were to appear in the 1911 and 1912 annual exhibitions of the Belfast Art Society.

It must have been during these years that he somehow managed to pay his own way to Paris, visiting museums and studying the Dutch and Italian masters to 'learn representational paintings', but, in art terms and financially, he found it so unprofitable that he returned home after only six months. Nevertheless, during his time abroad he was aware of new and challenging movements in art. Just before his arrival in Paris, Picasso had begun to cause a sensation with his 'cubist' style of painting and Conor, during his stay there, met the French artist André Lhote (1885–1962). According to Douglas Cooper in his book *The Cubist Epoch*, Lhote, who had previously painted in a sub-Impressionist manner, became one of the new recruits to the Cubist School of painting and began to show with the original group during 1911. By the summer of

7. Detail from *Five studies of the Female Head 1908–1914.* 19 February 1908. Pencil on paper.
19.1 × 14 cms
Linen Hall Library Collection, Belfast.

8. *The Fisherman.*
N.d. Pencil and watercolour
on paper.
30.5 × 24.1 cms
Miss Judith Wilson.

1912 a serious division of opinion developed in the Cubist group 'over
the question of whether realism or abstraction was the real goal of
Cubist painting. The principal champions of abstraction gathered in the
suburban studios at Puteaux of a mathematically and scientifically
minded trio of brothers: Jacques Villon, Marcel Duchamp and
Raymond Duchamp-Villon. The three brothers gave a scientific twist to
Cubism and drew into their circle a few kindred spirits', of whom Lhote
was one. It was in 1912, a year after discovering the work of Cézanne, that
Lhote 'was practicing an ineffective, mannered form of cubification. He
continued to work in this style for a year or two before establishing
himself, subsequently, in his writings as much as in his paintings, as
"the academician of Cubism" (Rosenblum).'

Many artists who had their own studios offered the use of these, for
several hours and for a small fee, to students who might wish to study
aspects of art, particularly modelling, and obtain guidance and advice
on their work. Conor recalled that Lhote was one of those who offered
this facility of which he took advantage, 'paying so much and working

9. *Eleventh Night.*
1912 approx. Crayon on paper.
38.1 × 30.5 cms
Ulster Folk Museum
Collection.

there for a couple of hours'.

Conor, however, was never one to jump on a band wagon and indeed regarded it as being very unwise to associate oneself with any fashionable novelty, since it might quickly go out of fashion. This attitude helped him to be, and to remain, true to himself all his life.

On his return from Paris he said, 'I showed what I did there at a local exhibition, then the interest began to take in my work. That was my beginning.' I have not been able to find any record of where the exhibition was held or the titles or number of works shown. It would have been interesting to have had some information about this. Certainly none of the picture titles listed in the Belfast Art Society catalogues for this period give any indication of having been French in subject or by influence.

It was not long before he resumed the work he loved best, the interpretation of the ordinary lives, the industries, the everyday affairs of his own Belfast people. He knew them and was one of them, understood their hopes, fears, courage, their kindliness, warmth and laughter. He felt that these were the people he could best depict in the impressionist style which he was to favour, perhaps because of the freedom of expression which it allowed him, unconfined by too much detail. The style was particularly suited to his crayon drawings and also allowed the imagination of the viewer to contribute to the appreciation of the work.

Although this style was still relatively unknown in Belfast, the pictures were admired by the people and drew praise in the newspapers; but it seems that few were purchased. Often those who best liked them

10. The Belfast Art Society
Outing at Belfast Castle 24
May 1913.
Conor is standing seventh
from the left.
Photograph from the Conor
papers.

were least able to afford them. Those who could have bought them, did not wish to be reminded, from inside their homes, of working conditions outside. Richard Valentine Williams, better known as Richard Rowley, poet and author of short stories and close friend of William Conor, wrote in his critical appreciation in Conor's book *The Irish Scene* that at an exhibition he advised a wealthy amateur to buy one of Conor's mill-worker drawings; the man's reply was, 'My wife doesn't like them things. She worked in a mill herself, and the neighbours might say yon was a portrait of her, when she was young.'

During these early years Padraic Woods, another local artist, remembers him as being something of a sport and recalls seeing a photograph in the Ulster Arts Club that had been taken on one of their outings; 'there was Billy Conor and another friend, Stanley Prosser, under a waterfall, probably in the Glens of Antrim, with the water coming down on both of them standing there in the altogether. It was just spontaneous, I suppose.' Although Conor said he was not really interested in sport he had kept three photographs taken during the third annual road walk from Belfast to Bangor, held on 20 May 1905, by David Allen and Sons 'for their employees'. There was also a card giving the names of the Committee, the judges and a list of the generous prizes ranging from a marble clock and bronze ornaments presented by the President, S. C. Allen, to a briar pipe and case. Conor also remarked to Herbert Bell that he had been 'in Trinity Harriers' and that he had attended Clifton Swimming Club; he recalled a photograph taken in the Club with 'me in front with arms folded pressing out biceps'.

In 1913, he was elected to the Committee of the Belfast Art Society Council.

# 3

# WAR ARTIST

Following the outbreak of the First World War in 1914 William Conor, as an official war artist, visited munition works and Army camps, such as Ballykinlar, and made many sketches, recording the everyday life of the soldiers of the Ulster Division. It was reported in the *Irish Times*, 9 August 1958, that on one of these visits to the training camp at Clandeboye in 1914, he had:

> arranged one evening to make a portrait of the Regimental Sergeant-Major, who prepared for the occasion by a lengthy session in the mess. While the sitting was in progress, he unsteadily picked up a hand grenade and mentioned as a point of interest that if he withdrew the pin at the top, he, the artist and the tent in which they sat would be blown sky high. Without questioning the truth of the statement, Conor went on, not quite as calmly as he could have wished, to make one of his best wartime drawings.

In fact Conor recalled that the Sergeant-Major actually had removed the pin but, happily, had replaced it while still holding the handle in position.

During Christmas week 1916, the Lord Mayor of Belfast, Sir Crawford McCullough, permitted the Parlour of the City Hall to be used for a one day viewing of a Conor Exhibition of crayon portrait drawings made directly from life at the various Ulster Division Training Camps. These thirty-three drawings were auctioned on the following day, 19 December, in the Mart, Stewart Street, off Cromac Square, by John Robinson & Co Ltd in aid of the Ulster Volunteer Force Hospitals; they realised well over £100. The exhibition included drawings of people identified with the Ulster Division and of many well known officers, such as the Rt Hon Sir Edward Carson, KC, MP, General Sir George Richardson, KCB and Lieutenant-Colonel James Craig, MP. These three drawings sold for seven guineas, five guineas and six guineas respectively.

Conor also made a pictorial illustration of the famous charge of the Ulster Division at Thiepval on 1 July 1916 which was sold for £4 14s 6d. Beautifully coloured prints of the picture for framing were to be had at 6d each and Christmas postcards of the same design at a penny each. The proceeds of the sale of the cards were also devoted to the UVF Hospital

11. Bugler, Ulster Division. 1916. Charcoal and red chalk on paper.
55 × 37.9 cms
Ulster Museum Collection, Belfast.

12. *Off, The Ulster Division.* 1915. Charcoal and red chalk on paper.
55 × 37.3 cms
Ulster Museum Collection, Belfast.

fund. The cards were sold at Robinson and Cleavers, Easons and other stationers in Belfast.

James Mackie, Chairman of the Belfast engineering firm James Mackie and Sons Ltd., in 1917 commissioned William Conor to make a drawing which would record his appreciation of the Belfast munition workers whom he had recruited for war work. The model chosen was Miss Madeleine Ewart, fourth daughter of Herbert Ewart (William Ewart and Son, Linen Manufacturers), who worked in the factory until her marriage at the end of that year to Philip Smiles, one of the 'self-help' family who became a director of the Belfast Ropeworks and later a Senate Member in the Northern Ireland Parliament. She is depicted

13. *Two Soldiers and a Girl.* N.d. Pencil and crayon on paper. 30 × 22.9 cms Ulster Museum Collection, Belfast.

14. *Fight and Endure.* 1914. Pencil and watercolour on paper. 35 × 24.3 cms Ulster Museum Collection, Belfast.

15. *'For Us'*, a colour postcard to raise money for the U.V.F. Hospital Fund. 1916. 13.9 × 8.9 cms Linen Hall Library Collection, Belfast.

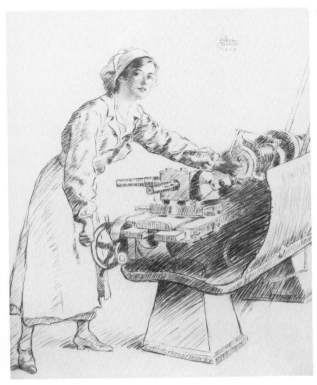 

operating a turret lathe which produced 18lb shrapnel shells.

Conor, who had been elected to the Committee of the Belfast Art Society in 1913, was made one of four Vice-Presidents in 1917, a position he held for one year.

In 1918 he had his work hung for the first time in the Royal Hibernian Academy (RHA), Dublin. Among the six works exhibited were a portrait of Major Peter Kerr Smiley MP, and a portrait of Lieutenant-Colonel Sir James Craig, Bart, MP.

The following year three works were hung at the RHA. The *Northern Whig* review of 2 April 1919 was not particularly appreciative:

Mr. Wm. Conor, a Belfast exhibitor, also departs from the accepted tradition in his two ambitious oil-paintings – "Mill-workers" (137) and "Brother and Sister" (191). He works almost entirely with the palette knife, and the general effect of his canvases is not unlike that of Hornel, the Scottish painter. But the colour, if vivacious, lacks brilliancy, and in the painting of the face of the girl in "Brother and Sister" one sees what Mr. Conor misses by sacrificing delicacy of texture to strength. The processional crowd of mill-girls is a happy conception, only one has the feeling that the artist saw the jumbled figures first and then as an afterthought added the houses on the hill to balance them. But the balance does not come quite right, and the composition is a little lob-sided. It has, however, a human interest, which one hopes Mr. Conor will develop to still greater effect in his work . . .

The review also mentions that a picture by Alfred Baker, as well as one by F. W. Hull and 'Mr. William Conor's dashing "Street Singers" (321) add to the attractiveness of the water-colour section'.

16

# 4

# LONDON: RECOGNITION
# AND
# RETURN TO BELFAST

Although Conor became better known after the war, times were still hard for him, and so early in 1921 he decided to go to London. Here he was often miserable; it was winter-time and his small room in 32 Percy Street, off the Tottenham Court Road, was bitterly cold. He said it was 'too cold to sleep'. Another Belfastman, E. M. O'Rorke Dickey, who had a room in the same building, advised Conor to line his canvas bed with brown paper or newspaper; 'I slept comfortably after that'. Even though Conor's stay in London was not long, he met most of the great figures in the London art circles, such as William Orpen, Wilson Steer and Augustus John, the latter sponsoring him for membership of the Chelsea Arts Club; his name does not, however, appear in the membership lists. Augustus John and Sir John and Lady Lavery were to become good friends to Conor. Sir John, a fellow Ulsterman, gave Conor much encouragement in his work and kind hospitality, and the friendship continued through meetings and correspondence. All these contacts were not only a great help to Conor in the art world, but gave his shy and retiring nature some social confidence.

Probably the most widely known story, certainly the one most often related, is that of Conor's introduction to Lady Lavery and it is the version told by the artist to Mercy Hunter which I use here.

Conor, who said of himself, 'I was very green, I was a wee green fellow,' was invited to Lady Lavery's salon. (This was the second Lady Lavery who was enormously tall, very beautiful and American, and whose lovely face was portrayed on the ten shilling Irish bank note for many years.) On his arrival at the Laverys' an intimidating butler opened the front door and ushered Mr William Conor into the Salon.

18. 32 Percy Street, London. Photograph: Arts Council of Northern Ireland.

Conor recalled, 'There was Lady Lavery lying on one of those chaise-longue, looking very, very beautiful and she put out a long languid hand and said, "How do you do". I shook it and said, "How do you do" and then I sat down. Then in came a marvellous young artist with a big bow tie and long floppy hair who went down on his knee, took the long languid hand, kissed it and said "Dear Lady, dear Lady". Man dear, was my face red!'

William Carter told me that this

. . . was a very important period of his life, indeed it had a great influence on him. He lived in what must have been a Bohemian type of area at that time because his lodgings had previously been occupied by Wyndham Lewis and before that again by some artist who had committed suicide; in fact, Willie said it was a ghostly place, there were manifestations. It was a time when he had little or no money and he would walk rather than take a bus, he had to, yet he was moving in circles where people had money, so he would find himself in the Café Royal very frequently and at parties. Augustus John was particularly good to him in taking him under his wing and drawing him out and, I think, helping him in all sorts of organisational ways and introducing him to people, so too was Sir John Lavery. He was very close indeed to Augustus John who always reproached him for 'the Presbyterianism' in his work; thought he would have been better without it.

This reproach by John may have arisen from a comment on his pictures made by Conor during his first visit by invitation to John's studio where he surveyed the canvasses. After long consideration he remarked in a strong Ulster dialect 'Mister John, there's only one thing wantin' in yer pictures.' 'What's that?' asked John. 'They have no Presbyterian feelin',' replied Conor gravely. (Reported by John South in *Everybody's Weekly*, 14 May 1927.)

Mercy Hunter recalls having heard a story about a social gathering at Augustus John's which also included William Orpen, Wilson Steer and William Conor, 'fresh from the country of the North of Ireland'.

Well, they had a tremendous evening and slept the rest of the night in John's Studio. The next morning they woke up with the most frightful heads, and looked at each other and Augustus John said, 'Huh! We're the people our mothers warned us against when we were coming to London'.

Many years later Conor spoke to William Carter of his love for a young French governess. One evening he took her out to dinner at the Café Royal, intending to propose marriage. However during the course of the meal a young man of his acquaintance joined them, uninvited, at the table; for the remainder of the evening it seems that conversation was confined to exchanges in French between the governess and the young man. As Conor was unable to understand or join in the conversation he said it made him realise how inadequate he was. The proposal of marriage was never spoken, and yet for the remainder of his life he always thought of her as being 'his girl' and that there could be no-one else.

For the 1921 Spring Exhibition of the London National Portrait Society four of his works were accepted. One of them was a portrait of the Prime Minister of the first Northern Ireland Parliament, Sir James Craig. Sir James offered fifteen guineas for the painting.

18

In May of that same year he held an exhibition of thirty pictures in pencil, crayon drawings and oil at the Dawson Gallery, 21 Dawson Street, Dublin. The *Freemans Journal* of 26 May picked out *The Little Guardian*, which was priced at ten guineas, and *The Edge of the Woods*, the most expensive work in the show at forty pounds, 'as two perfect gems in oils'. The prices of the drawings ranged from four to seven guineas, while seven of the eight oils ranged from ten to fifteen guineas.

On Conor's return to Belfast, he was appointed, at the suggestion of Sir John Lavery, to paint a pictorial record of the Opening of the First Northern Ireland Parliament by King George V on 22 June 1921, in the Council Chamber of Belfast City Hall. Before he received permission to proceed with the larger painting he had to review the criticisms which he received in a letter from the then Marquess of Dufferin and Ava, about his pastel sketch. Firstly, it was found that:

> . . . the figure of His Majesty is too broad in comparison with his height – it would do no harm to make him a little taller even if it is not true to life – Her Majesty shan't, I think, be represented in a hat as the ladies-in-waiting are in hats. The Members of the House of Commons must be facing His Majesty, even if it means that their faces cannot be seen.
>
> The colour of the coats of the parliamentary officers in the picture are not correct, they are too light a blue.
>
> I shall be so glad to give you all the assistance I can in the way of detail. I think that Sir F. Moneypenny's position in the picture, though not that which he actually occupied, should be retained. I think Lord Londonderry must be shown as sitting in the front bench of the Senate and not with the House of Commons Members.

19. *The Opening of the First Northern Ireland Parliament.* 1921. Oil on canvas. 90.5 × 140.4 cms Parliament Buildings Collection, Stormont, Belfast.

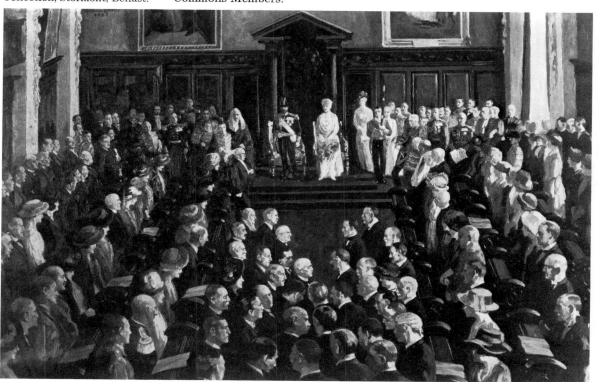

Conor used a black and white photograph which was to aid him greatly when he altered the positions of the Members of the House of Commons who directly faced His Majesty to the side view positions they now occupy in the finished picture, in spite of the advice of the Marquess.

It was the payment to Conor which made this a somewhat controversial picture. In 1922 he agreed to accept the £200 which, although a very unsatisfactory price, was all that the Committee felt they would be able to raise. However in May of the following year he received a cheque for only £131 6s 0d for the Parliamentary painting. Payment had been left to the generosity of the Members of Parliament and it was a great disappointment that only £91 6s 0d had been collected from the House of Commons and only £40 from the Senate. The insufficient amount which was collected cannot be excused. According to Lord Dufferin, even Captain Dixon, who collected for the House of Commons, had the greatest difficulty in getting the Members to subscribe at all and it was not because of any want of merit in the picture.

While the Parliament painting was in its early stages, Conor was also busy with other work at his studio in 7 Chichester Street, Belfast. This was a small studio on the third floor where the artist could work quietly and yet be conveniently in the city centre. He was to exhibit for the first time at the Royal Academy, London, from 2 May until 6 August and had the distinction of being placed on the line. The two pictures hung were portraits simply entitled *1820* and *Master H. W. R. Wallace* (the son of Colonel R. H. Wallace CB). In addition, his pictures *Young Girl and Child of Donegal* and *A Child of Ireland* were exhibited at the Société National des Beaux-Arts Salon de 1921, Paris. The art critic of *La Revue Moderne*, 30 October 1921, which illustrated in black and white Conor's pictures *Procession à Belfast* and *Dans la Rue*, hoped that the painter

would share his success between Ireland and France and that there would soon be further opportunities to view his work. He also received an invitation, which he accepted, from the Council of the Royal Glasgow Institute of the Fine Arts to send his work *Crayon Drawing of a Youth's Head* to their Sixtieth Annual Exhibition. This particular work had been chosen because it had been greatly admired by representatives of the Institute who had seen it at the Exhibition of the International Society of Painters, Sculptors and Gravers, London.

In this year a report of the Royal Society of Portrait Painters Annual Exhibition, in which Conor was included for the first time, appeared in the *Belfast Telegraph* of 23 December 1921. In it the writer quoted the art critic of the *Sunday Observer*, P. C. Konody, who had paid the artist a perceptive compliment about his portrait of R. V. Williams (Richard Rowley), having picked out this portrait for comment when many distinguished exhibitors were overlooked. He wrote:

> It is not among men of fashionable reputation that one has to look for the striking works of recent date. I do not remember having come across Mr. William Conor's work before, but his *R. V. Williams Esq.*; despite a certain harshness and brutality in the hatchet strokes of his brush, indicates gifts of a high order.

The same portrait attracted comment from the American press when it was hung in the Babcock Galleries, New York, in 1926:

> ... the suggestion of a lively, forceful vitality was more subtly portrayed in the bust portrait of Richard Rowley, a silver-haired man with a powerful head and face that lose nothing of that quality in Mr. Conor's canvas.

On 18 November 1921 Sir John Lavery, in a letter to Conor, had written:

> You have scored a success at the Royal Portrait Society your work looks so much better than it did in Belfast and I have been asked to propose you for membership which I would be very pleased to do should you decide to stand.

Sir John followed this up with a second letter (2 December) advising Conor that he had 'asked the Secretary of the Royal Society of Portrait Painters to put your name in the list of candidates with me as proposer and that of Richard Jack as seconder'. The Secretary had already sent Conor an application form for completion and return so that his name could be officially listed; this form which remains blank is with his papers and there is no indication as to why nothing more seems to have been done about it.

Another letter which he received at the end of this year from Sir John suggested that if the *Twelfth* picture were free he should send it, plus a couple of drawings, to the 'World Congress of the Irish Race', a small collection of pictures by Irish Artists, to be exhibited at the Galerie Barbazanges, Paris, from 20 January until 20 February 1922. This he did, exhibiting the *Twelfth* under the title of *Le Cortège Orangiste à Belfast*.

The principal exhibitors at the exhibition were Sean Keating, M. Harry Clarke, Jack B. Yeats, Sir John Lavery, Paul Henry, E. M. O'R. Dickey, George Russell (A.E.), D. Bond Walker, William Leech, Miss

22. *The Bridal Morning.*
1923 approx. Pencil and
crayon.
54 × 44.4 cms
The City Art Gallery
Collection, Manchester.

Eva Hamilton; other artists, including Conor, were Patric Tuohy, Leo
Whelan, G. Kelly, Walter Osborne, Dermod O'Brien, Grace Henry (first
wife of Paul Henry), Mary Swanzy, Estella Solomons and Sarah Purser.
Sculptors who exhibited were Albert Power and M. Oliver Sheppard.

It was reported in *Le Temps* Paris, 21 April 1922, that a portrait, *Poète
irlandais*, by Conor was hung at the Paris Salon for that year and
showed 'a decision, a frankness of touch which one seldom sees'.

The 'Colour Magazine' Exhibition of Modern Art which ran from 29
March until 12 April 1922, at the Grosvenor Galleries, London, included
Conor's oil painting *The Lost Child*. The 'Conor' exhibition catalogue
produced by John Magee's Gallery, Belfast for 22 October 1923,
included exerpts from past press reviews, one of which, by P. C. Konody,
Art Critic for the *Observer*, had said of this painting when it was
exhibited at the Grosvenor Galleries that 'Mr William Conor, a young
Belfast painter, displays remarkable talent in *The Lost Child*, a scene of
Irish village life, in which the tone-quality of the buildings and sky
could scarcely be excelled.'

The Grosvenor Galleries Annual Summer Exhibition for 1922
included Conor's drawing *The Street Preacher* while his oil *At The Half-
Door* was hung at their annual Winter Exhibition.

During this year an exhibition of his work was held at John Magee's
Donegall Square West Gallery, Belfast. Here were included pictures of

mill-workers, a labour meeting in the shipyards and an Orange Procession of the Twelfth of July.

Conor received a letter dated 8 February 1923, from the Director of 'Galerie de Marsan', 6 Rue des Pyramides, Paris, inviting the artist, whom he had not met but whose work he knew, to exhibit a group of his pictures in his new gallery, where he was arranging shows for the coming season, preferring the work of painters who showed real personality. Unfortunately, due to other commitments at this time Conor was unable to accept.

It is always fascinating to find comments made by an artist about his own pictures, so it is interesting to note the details that Conor gave to Lawrence Haward of the Manchester Art Gallery when, in 1923, they purchased from him three pencil and crayon drawings for their permanent collection: *Maternal Love*, *The Cronies*, and *The Bridal Morning*, a sketch for an oil painting *The Wedding* which was reproduced in the art magazine *Colour* (Nov/Dec Vol. 19.4–5 1923). Conor wrote:

> The subject for 'Cronies' was found in a narrow street through which I was passing in the early forenoon. Two neighbours who have 'redded up' the house, after their lords have left for the factory or the ship-yard, are having a [*sic*] amicable chat before confronting their arduous labours of the kitchen.
>
> 'The Bridal Morning' is an impression of a wedding party just leaving the bride's home, after the wedding breakfast. That the bridegroom is a well-to-do-artisan is indicated by the fact that he can afford to have a 'taxi' for the wedding journey, whilst the cheerful interest shown by the assembled crowd of neighbours, is proof that even in a dingy city street 'all the world loves a lover'.
>
> 'Maternal Love' is, of course, a universal subject. Nothing is more striking in the life of an industrial city like Belfast, than the affection and care lavished by the working class women upon their off-spring. As far as love can provide it, a poor child has just a [*sic*] good chance of happiness, as the child of a wealthy home.
>
> As to the technical side of these drawings, I try to keep myself as free from theory as possible, I use the pencil or coloured crayons, just as the fancy moves me. Perhaps in a drawing of much detail like the 'Bridal Morning' I prefer to use the pencil – whilst in a subject which demands broader treatment, I find myself more at home with the crayon – but it is all a question of the mood and, if the inspiration is urgent enough I do not think it matters greatly to me, which method is adopted.

These three pictures were shown at an exhibition of his work held at the Collector's Gallery, Manchester, in March of 1923. The following month the exhibition was shown at the Goupil Gallery, London, and on 24 May 1923, that same Gallery opened an exhibition, paintings and drawings, at which Conor exhibited thirteen pencil and crayon drawings and thirty oil paintings. A comprehensive review of this one-man show appeared in the magazine *Colour* (Nov/Dec 1923 Vol. 19 No. 4–5 pp 10–12). It mentions that this exhibition 'introduced to London the works of an Irish artist who, up to the present, has been known only to a small circle of friends and admirers'. Six pictures were selected for particular comment on the artist's differing interpretations of several

human emotions. The review indicates a sympathy with, and understanding of, Conor's approach:

> The reaction of the life-struggle in a manufacturing community upon the
> individual is nearly always the basis on which his art is founded. This idea
> pervades that fine painting 'The Launch' one of his most recent achievements.
> Here the interest does not centre on the spectacle of the great ship sliding
> magnificently down the slips, but on the figures of the three shipyard workers
> who watch intently the seal of final success set upon their labours . . .

23. *The Launch*.
1923. Oil on canvas.
76.2 × 50.8 cms sight
Private collection.

The comedy of city life does not escape Mr. Conor's observation. There is rich and kindly humour in 'The House across the Street' in which he paints two women looking from their doorway upon the actions of their opposite neighbours, whilst in 'The Melodeon Player' he chooses for his subject the joyousness of a group of young people who move along the pavement to the sound of the cheerful music . . . Another aspect of city life is recorded in 'The Old Clothes Seller' in which the incidents and background of a market for old clothes are used to make an interesting and impressive composition. The figures of the two women who are haggling over the price of a garment are simply and strongly designed, and in the calculating pose and demeanour of the prospective purchaser all the caution and foresight of the Ulster-Scot type have been studied and expressed.

This power to build up and suggest character in his subjects, is one which makes for Mr. Conor's success as a portrait painter. An admirable example of his method will be found in 'The Minister' a portrait of a clergyman, handled with great sincerity and straight-forwardness. [This is possibly a self-portrait in clerical robe.] The solidity of the painting, and the strong drawing and brushwork with which the modelling of the features is achieved, make this a very striking and memorable piece of work. But in this class of painting 'The White Door' is perhaps the artist's greatest triumph. Here he has set for himself a difficult task. The figure of a young girl is placed against a white door, which she has just slightly opened and, with one hand upon the handle, she turns to face the spectator. The drawing of the hand and arm which are stretched out to open the door is very well handled, whilst the rich yet subdued flesh-tints of the piquant face are admirably contrasted with the tones of the yellow jumper, which the subject is wearing. To adjust all these colours and tones against the dead-white of the door, and to bring out the solidity of the figure against such a background, was a task which might have daunted a less resolute man, but Mr. Conor has conquered all these difficulties, and has succeeded in doing so without any appearance of straining his method or his medium. There is nothing forced either in pose or execution, all is simple and straight-forward, and one leaves the picture with the sensation of having seen a gracious and elegant movement, deftly and convincingly displayed.

(This could be the picture which is among the Linen Hall Library Collection, Belfast.)

Conor was again represented at the 1923 Paris Salon with three works, *Testing His Wings*, *Young Mill Worker*, and *Strollin' Home*. In October, John Magee's Gallery in Belfast held an exhibition of his paintings and drawings. It was reported in the *Northern Whig and Belfast Post* (23 October 1923), that it was the first time that admirers in his native city had had an opportunity of seeing a representative exhibition of his works. Among the oil paintings shown were *The Darlins, The House across the Street*, a fine portrait of Lady Mabel Annesley and *The Launch*, which the art critic of the *Whig* thought to be 'perhaps the finest picture in the exhibition, perhaps even the finest picture ever painted with a modern commercial enterprise for subject'.

Lady Mabel Annesley, herself an artist who had spent a year studying wood engraving at the Central School of Arts, London from 1920–1921, often sent her woodcuts to Conor for his opinion, criticism and advice. Conor also appreciated the encouragement she gave him, especially when in 1921 he painted her portrait, a picture which he regarded as

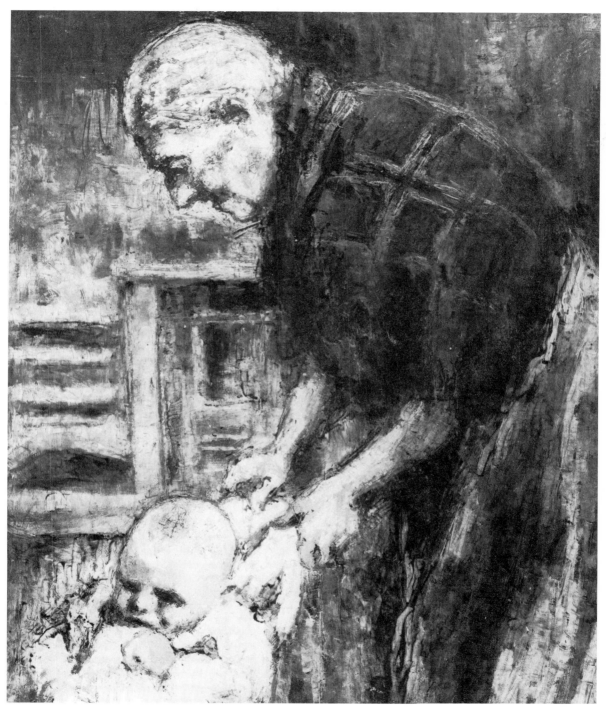

24. *Testing his Steps.*
1920 approx. Oil on canvas.
50.8 × 40.6 cms
Ulster Folk Museum
Collection.

being 'our painting'. The portrait is the frontispiece to Lady Mabel's unfinished autobiography *As the Sight is Bent* (Museum Press, London, 1964).

The late Richard Hayward, in a critical appreciation in the *Ulster*

*Review* for October 1924, wrote:

> William Conor is one of the most strongly individualised painters of to-day, and he has made it possible for one to say this, not so much by his rigid adherance to a peculiar subject matter, as by a most extraordinary apartness of line which is almost ferocious in its primitive strength. This quality is easily recognisable through the whole series of his work, but you will find it most marked in his drawings . . . It reminds one of nothing so much as the technique of the stonecutter filtered through the mind and hand of an authentic artist. All the swift chisel strokes and the deft impacts of the mallet are there . . .
>
> He has discovered the harmony of colour and the grace of draping and movement in the shawls of our mill-workers; he has captured the terrifying wit and repartee of a group of 'shawlies' homeward-bound, and has even confined within his line the running commentary which these same ladies utter on the peculiarities of dress, gait, and gesture of their passers-by; he has shown the love of the submerged mother for her child, and the care which the 'big sister' bestows upon the later offspring of her parents. It is perhaps in pastel and hard crayon that William Conor finds the most perfect medium for the expression of this side of his virile genius . . .
>
> . . . Art is no circumscribed thing . . . he is fast becoming known as a portrait painter. All his painting has in it the swift analytical quality which inheres in all genuine artistic creation and this is particularly marked in his portrait work.

Although portraiture was never to take first place in his work, Conor proved himself to be a perceptive and very capable artist in this medium, and at times the results are very fine. The man who could assess shrewdly the qualities of a human being was remarkably well able to interpret these in paint, although he himself admitted to the difficulties of this art form.

It is to Conor's credit that Sir John Lavery had suggested he should be approached to undertake the Northern Ireland Parliamentary painting in 1921, which was, of course, group portraiture, and that shortly afterwards Sir John had been invited to propose William Conor for membership of the Royal Society of Portrait Painters.

For Conor himself there was always the difference between the spontaneity of the 'quick sketch' portrait as in his folk studies – not always anatomically correct – and the more serious formality of the commissioned portrait in which veracity to the subject was of importance. Another point might be made. The formal portrait is usually commissioned for a private client, to be hung in the sitter's home, or for presentation to an individual on retirement, or as representative of a public body or holder of public office. In such cases the portrait is rarely seen by the general public, whereas an artist's other work is exhibited to a wider audience. I have been struck by the quality of the drawing of hands in several of his portraits, conveying delicacy, strength, the languid hand, the hands of hearth and home, adding something to the interpretation of the sitter's personality. I think particularly of the hands holding a pair of spectacles in the portrait of *Thomas A. Montgomery DL, JP* (in the possession of Armagh County Museum); those in the portraits of *Eleanor* (also

25. *'1825'*. (A self portrait.)
1920 approx. Oil on canvas.
54.6 × 37.8 cms sight
Ulster Museum Collection,
Belfast.

entitled *The Black Frock* and in the possession of the Linen Hall
Library, Belfast), *Blanche Bennett* and an interior scene showing an
elderly woman (probably Conor's mother) seated in a chair with a shawl
about her shoulders.

It is obvious that Conor's own interest in portraiture was sufficiently
strong to encourage him to make many self sketches and portraits –
perhaps for practice, perhaps because by sketching himself he did not
have to pay others to act as life models. But the most compelling reason
for his interest was that commissions for portraits represented his most
secure source of income. Some of his self portraits are: *1825, The Studio
Dance* (in which the artist is the melodeon player), *The Melodeon Player*
(detail from *The Studio Dance*), the artist wearing the clerical gown of a

Presbyterian minister, *The Crotal Coat*, another oil painting which may have been suggested by a photograph of Conor when he was a Vice-President of the Belfast Art Society in 1917. This photograph and another taken of the Society's outing to Airfield House, also in 1917, are the only two which I have come across in which he is featured with a moustache. Other self portraits are *The Gombeen Man*, several untitled head and shoulder studies in crayon, and the oil of the artist wearing his gown as Honorary Master of Arts. An early press report commented that 'unlike many artists, he does not despise the quality of getting a likeness'.

During 1924 Conor was to become a member of the Belfast Art Society Dramatic Club, which recently had been established as a branch of the Belfast Art Society for the purpose of increasing knowledge and appreciation of dramatic art by presenting plays and readings. Although Conor took part, he felt that he 'was not good at theatricals'.

26. *The Studio Dance.*
1924. Oil on canvas.
128.3 × 101.6 cms
Linen Hall Library Collection,
Belfast.

27. 'Come to Ulster, it's Jolly!'
This painting was to be
reproduced as a poster for the
Ulster Tourist Development
Association.
Reproduced from the *Northern
Whig and Belfast Post*, 26
January 1926.

In Dublin, the St Stephen's Green Gallery held, in 1924, an exhibition which consisted of forty-five of Conor's works, oils, water-colour, pen, pencil and crayon drawings. Among those exhibited were *The Weavers*, the self-portrait *Painter and Melodeon* and *The Patchwork Quilt*. During the period of this exhibition Conor was informed by the Royal Academy, London, that his three paintings, *The Studio Dance*, *At The Door* and *The Black Gown* had been accepted, although *The Studio Dance* was the only one hung. Also in London his picture *The Red Haired Boy* was hung at the Royal Society of Portrait Painters.

Writing from Sydney, Australia, in *Ireland's Saturday Night* in January 1924, J. K. Waring referred with pleasure to an exhibition of European pictures held there in 1923 and in which were hung three works by William Conor including *At The Door*.

In the following year the St Stephen's Green Gallery again mounted a large representative exhibition consisting of fifty pictures, thirteen oils, fourteen water-colour and twenty-three pen, pencil and crayon drawings. Among those shown were *Mirth*, *The Darlin'*, *The Kiss*, *The Sulky Child*, *The Black Shawl*, *Window Sill*, *The Launch*, *Motherhood*, *Love Bird* and two portraits, one of a Belfast lady (Miss Blanche Bennett, painted in 1924), and the other, kindly lent for the occasion, a head and shoulders study done in conté crayon, of a Dublin lady (the Honourable Lady de Courcy Wheeler).

Members of the Press were invited to a private viewing on 25 January 1926, in the Classic Cinema, Belfast, of a poster painted by Conor for the Tourist Development Association. Conor's idea behind this poster, as reported in that day's *Belfast Telegraph*, was:

> . . . to get as far away as possible from the conventional Irish poster of shawled peasant, white-washed, thatched cottage, and brown, melancholy bog. The tourist did not come to Ulster to weep over the sorrows of Dark Rosaleen. Besides, Dark Rosaleen in the North had dried her tears long ago, and had a smile on her face, and very often wore silk stockings. Her house, or rather her father's house, was up-to-date. The visitor did not come here to rough it in discomfort.

The reported description of the poster was sympathetic:

> Health and vigour, bracing air, and roaming mountain stream, and far-stretching beach were the dominant notes of Ulster. His background was a composite suggestion of all those things, taken from not one watering-place or tourist district, but suggesting the infinite variety of Ulster's scenery as a whole.
>
> In the foreground he has placed two little girls leaping and gambolling with mere joy of life; no dolled-up misses for an asphalt parade or a jazz band, but healthy, happy children enjoying a holiday, life-joyous little animals, escaped from the conventions and restraints of city life; living for a while among the glen and hill and slopes of Ulster, the way children should live their whole childhood.

The posters when reproduced from Conor's design were to be displayed on specially allocated positions over the entire railway systems of Great Britain.

# 5

# AMERICA

Conor was again elected, in 1926, as one of four Vice-Presidents of the Belfast Art Society.

Yet times remained hard. He still found it difficult to make a living and in June 1926 accepted an invitation from the Advertising Club of Ulster which included him among the British delegates who left Southampton on 12 June aboard the Cunarder *Berengaria*, for the Philadelphia Convention of the World's Advertising Club. Although he did not greatly like America his reaction was, 'Now that I'm here, I might as well stay and make money'. Several of his friends thought that he might perhaps decide to remain there, but he said, 'No – I'd rather be a poor man in Belfast than a rich man here.'

He took note of the friendly advice he received from Sir John Lavery that Americans must be bluffed and stayed for three or four days in the most expensive hotel in Philadelphia. There, as he anticipated, he was 'discovered' by a lady reporter of the *Ledger*.

The article in the *Philadelphia Ledger* of 21 June 1926 describes how, as he sat in the lobby of the Bellevue-Stratford Hotel before going to meet the Mayor, he appeared perplexed and also very amused:

What delighted Mr. Conor most yesterday morning was the women who filled the lobby. 'They are so tall and slender', he commented, 'so much taller than our women. I would like to pick out one right now and paint her.' The American girl he sees with very different eyes. 'She is so unlike the Irish girl', he explained, 'the Irish are sturdy and they work so hard'.

The dash across country from the boat to Philadelphia must have added to what he regarded the most mystifying thing about America –

28. *Riveting.*
1940. Watercolour on paper.
45.5 × 35.5 cms
Ulster Museum Collection,
Belfast.

the rush. 'You really don't get any further than we do! You only look as
though you are doing more – we never hurry like this.'

The *Ledger* reporter expected him, after attending the advertising
convention, to undertake 'a leisurely trip through Connecticut country,
an exhibition or two and a couple of portraits'. In fact, he spent the
remainder of that summer in Ridgefield, Connecticut, staying with a
former Ulsterman and Rector of the Parish Church there, the Reverend
W. B. Lusk and his family.

In September of that year Conor was back in New York where in the
following month he held an exhibtion of 'Irish Life', in the Babcock
Galleries. The exhibition included *The Accordion Player, Cronies, At
The Pump* and *The Wedding*. A report published in the American press
on 3 October 1926 made the point that 'All these canvases are painted in
a very personal color scheme that harks back to the solidities of the
Italian school of the late Renaissance rather than that of the
contemporary school with which one might expect him to be associated'.

Also included were two portraits, that of *Richard Rowley Esq.*, and
*The 7th Marquess of Londonderry*, a portrait with which the Marquess
himself was not at all pleased. It was only because he was anxious that
Conor's visit to America should prove successful, that he gave his
consent for it to be taken. The portrait, listed at a price of $1,000, was not
sold and was eventually brought back to Belfast. It stayed in Conor's
keeping for some considerable time during which he made some
alterations in the tones, 'which my friends tell me result in a great
improvement and is a much better likeness of your Lordship'. Later it
was acquired by The Queen's University of Belfast, of which Lord

29. *Men of the Home Front.*
(Shipyard workers crossing
Queen's Bridge, Belfast.)
1940. Crayon on paper.
37.8 × 54.2 cms
Ulster Museum Collection,
Belfast.

Londonderry had been a former Chancellor.

A different opinion however was given in the same American press report of 3 October:

As a portrait painter Mr. Conor strikes an even sturdier note than in his studies of his fellow townsmen of a social order less exalted than the subjects of his two likenesses. The three-quarters standing figure of the Marquis of Londonderry in his university robes is a capital piece of painting and even finer as a character study, the figure and head being admirably modeled and full of the suggestion of a lively, forceful vitality . . .

Few are the portrait painters that have come to us from abroad in recent years that have so much to say for themselves in good, sound work as William Conor, of Belfast.

Sir John and Lady Lavery were also in New York at this time, staying at the Commodore Hotel. While Conor was waiting in the foyer to see them he was warmly greeted by a gentleman whom he did not immediately recognise. This was the writer and poet Osbert Sitwell, with whom he had dined a short time before in London. Sitwell complimented Conor on the success of his exhibition adding that his own series of lectures in New York was not proving as successful as he had hoped.

The picture shown at the Babcock, *At the Pump*, was later bought and presented to the Brooklyn Museum by Sir John Lavery. Conor recalled an amusing incident about this picture:

As I was standing at the pump in the little village of Greencastle near Belfast, waiting for the children to come along, I was in a sort of reverie with my head

34

down and quietly tapping the street with my stick. Suddenly, someone caught me by the arm and a kindly voice said, 'Can I help you across the street, my poor fellow?' I had actually been mistaken for a blind man.

In New York he was invited to be a guest at some university and was assured he would not have to make a speech. However, half-way through the afternoon it was suggested that, 'Perhaps Mr. Conor would say a few words'. At that moment a good story came to mind:

I was going to bow right and left and sit down again. I told them that this reminded me of a story I knew of Mrs. Patrick Campbell, the famous actress. On one occasion when she met a very famous literary man, she said to him [that] very often when talking to her friends she found great difficulty in knowing where to place her colons and semi-colons, and he said this wasn't his difficulty. His difficulty was knowing what to put in between them.

Conor's youngest brother, Martin, who was already living in America and continued to do so for a number of years, wrote a letter to Conor dated 7 October 1926, from Boston, Massachusetts, explaining that he was unable to have the Monday off and did not feel it worthwhile to visit him in New York. He advised him to 'go ahead with your plans for a week-end with Hunniford. It will do you more good anyway to get away from New York for a few days. I don't blame you for wanting to get away from it, for a while'.

In February of the following year the Brooklyn Museum held an 'Exhibition of Water Color Paintings, Pastels and Drawings by American and European Artists', from which they acquired Conor's *Youth and Age*. His pictures also went on view at the American Irish Historical Society's building in New York.

Amongst the portraits he painted during his stay in New York was one of the Reverend Father John H. Dooley, apparently a popular priest of the Roman Catholic Church, who was founder of Corpus Christi Parish and the Pastor from 1906 until his death in 1934.

It was while in America that he was asked why he spelled his name with one 'n' when it was usually spelt with two. He replied with a smile, 'Oh, I suppose some of my ancestors found some difficulty in making the two "n's" meet, so they dropped one'. This story served as a rather delightful explanation since, in fact, only William had made this change; the rest of the family had continued to spell the name Connor.

Conor occasionally met Joseph Campbell, the Belfast born poet and fellow member of the Ulster Arts Club, whose very fine woodcut designs can be seen illustrating his poems in *Earth of Cualann* published in 1917. The meeting place was a restaurant in Washington Square, New York, and here they would talk on many subjects. According to Conor, Campbell was having a lean time conducting what he called 'The School of Irish Studies' on the top floor of a building at 6 East 12th Street, Fifth Avenue, teaching Irish Language, dance and song. This was Campbell's second visit to America and sometime after his meetings with Conor in 1927 he was appointed to the Staff of Fordham University as Professor of Irish Literature. Even though he returned to Ireland in July, 1939, the opportunity did not arise for Joseph Campbell and Conor to meet again.

During Conor's stay in New York he became friendly with a priest who bought some of his paintings and obtained a commission for him to paint a well known person in the city. On one occasion when the priest, whom he did not name, visited Conor as he was working:

A very interesting over-dressed young man entered. After his leaving, the priest, he says to me, 'that's a most famous bootlegger,' he says, 'that's the most famous bootlegger if you know what a bootlegger means . . .' Anyhow [he] was the most famous bootlegger in New York, 'and if you could get him to paint your portrait [sic] he would give you a blank cheque', and er . . . However, I saw no more . . . they tell me he was called the Baron of Broadway. I saw no more of the Baron of Broadway but I remember about six months or maybe more – I was home then and I read somewhere in our papers that the Baron of Broadway was what you might call 'put on the spot' at that time, you know the antagonism between one group and another and er ha ha . . . he was shot up. I was thinking maybe it was just as well I didn't paint his portrait 'cause they killed all the evidence too.

Before leaving America after his extended visit Conor, in an unidentified American newspaper report, expressed his views that the country was 'in danger of losing her soul through materialism'.

Your labour saving devices, tend to standardise to the point of sameness and to create a dearth not only of original thought but also of local color and of the human activities which make any single country in Europe a thrilling experience to the seeker after inspiration. The various parts of America, by reason of your modern institutions, are becoming more and more one in point of view in the increasing sameness of life.

Conor later wrote an article entitled 'My American Impressions' which appeared in *Ulster Life and Opinion* on 26 May 1927. In it he stated that:

New York, as a modern city, would assuredly not take first place in a beauty competition; but its new architecture, or rather engineering, is giving to it a new shape and form which is certainly original and impressing. New York will be a great city when finished, but Lord knows when that will be. The New Yorker is for ever striving after bigness. He loves big things, and no sooner is a colossal building erected than another slightly smaller one is pulled down and replaced by a still greater colossus. Side by side with this craze for big buildings is the American's insatiable craving for the antique.

New York is full of so called curio shops, and on going further afield I was amazed to find at least one antique shop in every small village. Over there The Old Master hunt has become quite an obsession; in fact a friend laughingly informed me that the Old Master Industry was one of New York's staple concerns.

Architecturally, I must confess New York did not impress me. In a moment of frankness I unburdened my impressions in the presence of a Press representative. I told her that New York was too material, too mechanical, to be beautiful or artistic. The following morning, on opening the *New York World*, I was horrified to see a heavily printed streamer running right across the front page – 'Artist Conor Chides Americans on Materialism.' Needless to say I was very careful in subsequent interviews.

The New York buildings are the direct outcome of the Zoning Laws, introduced in 1916, which stipulate that every new structure must not rise higher than the width and a half of the street or avenue in which it is to be erected. After this height is reached a step back is made, so many more stories

30. *At the Pump.*
1926 approx. Oil on canvas.
61.3 × 47.8 cms
The Brooklyn Museum
Collection, New York. (A
gift of Sir John Lavery.)

added; another few yards back, another few stories added; and so on until a pyramid-like pinnacle scrapes the sky. Certainly these new buildings are a great improvement on the old skyscrapers which, according to Pennell, resembled huge packing cases.

The American Eve seems to get more out of life than the American Adam. The poor fellow invariably wears a drawn and gum-chewing expression, and his poor thin limbs show signs of the wear and tear of that perpetual New

York hustle. He certainly is a live wire and looks it.

Now Miss America is another proposition. She is beautifully dressed, and dearly loves a good time. It matters not the amount of clothes necessary for New York's cold winter, or lack of clothes in the warm summer, Miss New York will be always smartly dressed. Comfort before everything is her motto in summer, and she appears indifferent whether you are shocked or not. She agrees with Shakespeare that 'All the world's a stage,' and uses lip stick, rouge and powder ad lib, in public, and generally at meal times. How to 'make up' gracefully in public seems to be an essential part of the American girl's education.

Apropos American girls. At dinner one evening I mentioned to my fair companion that I thought American girls very chic. Horror of horrors – Next morning a New York paper flaunted the following full page streamer – 'Irish Artist Stunned by American Girls' Beauty.'

One rarely meets old people in New York. Where they go is a puzzle. Is it a case of the survival of the fittest, or, terrible thought, is Father Time defied successfully, and was that delightfully vivacious young lady you had to a Broadway show really a great grandmother? I wonder.

On the whole the New Yorker is a very amiable and obliging person. Even the traffic 'cop' may leave his point duty to take your arm and saunter off with you to find your destination. The disadvantage of this proffered kindness is to make one feel, especially a Belfast man, that he is being 'Tuk up to the office.'

The overhead railways, trolly-cars, the pulling down and putting up of buildings, all tend to make New York the noisiest city in the world, and at first unbearable to the stranger. The mechanical jangle and racket is 'the limit'. Of course every mechanical aid to production is used in America; by the aid of machines everything is worked scientifically and automatically. To enter a subway you place a nickel in one of the many turnstiles, which are all clattering hideously. When your train arrives the doors open automatically, and you, with many others, automatically walk in and take a seat, providing there is one, which is hardly likely. However, one can pleasantly pass the time, especially if you are artistically inclined, by standing and watching the faces of your fellow-passengers taking on extraordinary shapes in their efforts to chew gum.

To an Ulsterman, White Street, Franklin Street, and parts of Fifth Avenue, are the most homeish places in New York. On every side one sees many familiar names of well-known Ulster business houses. To the home-sick Ulsterman I know of no better tonic than a stroll down one of these streets. Many names could be mentioned of Ulstermen prominent in the business life of New York – Robert McBratney, Sam Richardson, Henry Thompson, are but a very few. The founder of the greatest dry goods store was an Ulsterman – Mr. A. T. Stewart. One of the most palatial buildings in Fifth Avenue, with its wonderful shop fronts, is owned by three Ulster brothers – John, Charles and James McCutcheon.

On coming home I spent my first few days in a Co. Down village. I awoke one sunny morning to hear the hen cackling in the yard, and then, most glorious of all sounds (after the racket of New York) the rumpety-bump-bump of an Irish country cart rumbling over the cobbles. After all, there's no place like Ireland.

# 6

# RETURN TO IRELAND

On the 12 March 1927, Conor sailed from New York for England aboard the *S.S. Asconia* and on his return to Belfast he obtained a new studio at 26b Prudential Chambers, Wellington Place. Before his return, 'A Loan Exhibition of Irish Portraits by Ulster Artists' had been opened on 2 February, by Mrs Hugh O'Neill at the Belfast Municipal Museum and Art Gallery, in which the only portrait by Conor was a crayon drawing of *Dion*, the young son of Richard Hayward, who had lent the picture.

Mercy Hunter's earliest memory of William Conor was at the Empire Ball held at the Plaza in Belfast on 24 May 1927; those who wished could go in fancy dress. Members of the Ulster Arts Club decided upon an Egyptian theme and Mercy Hunter 'was carried in on a great palanquin by four painters; my brother John F. Hunter, Padraic Woods, Rendal Wood and William Conor'.

Apart from designing the cover of the official programme for British Empire Week which began on 23 May, Conor also held an Empire Exhibition, comprised of forty-five pictures, at his studio in Wellington Place, Belfast. Among the oil works were *The Melodeon Player*, *Cronies*, *Gossip*, *The Reader*, *Study*, a woman reading, *The Fortune Teller*, *The Sulky Child* and *The Fiddler*. Among the crayon works was a sketch of Professor Meredith, *Dutchie* (a head and shoulder study of Dutchie Torney), *Swing Boats* and a watercolour, *Queen's Bridge*.

In 1928 he submitted to the City of Manchester Queen's Park Art Gallery, his picture *The Donkey Cart*, for their exhibition 'Pictures with a Subject'.

It was reported in an unnamed newspaper article that Conor had been requested by the Committee of the Royal National Eisteddfod of Wales,

31. *Homewards.*
1925 approx. Crayon on paper.
40.6 × 30.5 cms
Ulster Folk Museum
Collection.

which was being held that year at Treorchy, to forward two pictures for
their exhibition in the art section. This he did, sending a character
study, *The Cellist*, and *The Launch*. The exhibition was 'composed solely
of the works of master painters' and included pictures by 'Sir William
Goscombe, R.A., Sir Frank Shortt, R.A., Augustus John, R.A., William
Strang, R.A., Muirhead Bone, Laura Knight and Baron d'Erlanger'.
Surprisingly, there is no reference to Conor's work in either the
Programme or the Catalogue of the 1928 Eisteddfod.

This year saw the publication by Ernest Benn, London, of *Robes of
Thespis*, costume designs by modern artists. Illustrated under the

section 'Irish Dramatic Costume' were five Conor sketches:

Plate 46, for Gerald MacNamara's *Thompson in Tir-na-n-Óg*, Ulster
  Players, Belfast;
Plate 47, 'Nance' for Richard Rowley's *The Last Coyne of Killehalla*,
  Northern Drama League, Belfast;
Plate 48, for Peter Maginnes's *The Old Women*;
Plate 49, for Richard Rowley's *The Last Coyne of Killehalla*, Northern
  Drama League, Belfast;
Plate 50, for Rutherford Mayne's *The Drone*;

Of the five sketches only Plate 46 was in colour; this and Plates 49 and
50 were signed William W Conor.

### The eye of the beholder.

In April 1929 the Godfrey Phillips Galleries in London held an
exhibition of forty-five of Conor's drawings, some of which were in
colour. It was here in his opening speech that Conor expressed his
critical opinions of the fashions of the day, and his regret at the passing
of the use of the shawl. These remarks were to bring him wide press
coverage (there were even photographs in the newspapers of well
known film actresses wearing shawls which had been superimposed
upon their heads) and much personal correspondence. I feel Conor's
reply should be quoted in full since, from his long study of people in their
different settings, his own words are a splendid confirmation of what
can be seen in his pictures.

Since making my plea that women should discard that abomination of to-day,
the modern hat, and adopt the shawl, I have been inundated with letters.
Many from girls in Mayfair as well as Whitechapel have upbraided me; while
one enterprising millinery establishment has offered me a contract to design
not only headgear but frocks.

Of course, I had to refuse. I am only a portrait painter and know little of
such things except how they appear to me; and to me they appear mighty bad!
My main quarrel with the modern woman's dress is that it looks so vulgarly
new, just as if it had come straight from the band-box or shop-window. I am not
trying to argue in favour of a race of tramp women in bedraggled, dirty attire.
What I mean is this. A woman has a gown made. It is strongly stamped with the
personality of its creator, however much he may protest that it was specially
designed to suit the purchaser.

Just when the gown is getting accustomed, if I might use the term, to the
wearer, and her personality is shown in it by wearing, she discards it. Silk, for
example, will only cling lovingly on a beautiful arm when it is used to the
curves of that arm.

Thus we seldom see our women folk as themselves. Perhaps they don't want
us to. They are part this hairdresser, that dressmaker, and the other beauty
specialist. Personality is being crushed out by the women themselves just at
that period of history when, still exalted with emancipation, they still have
most.

If every woman had different clothes designed for her the horror of the
modern trend would not be so great. Even if some of the styles were definitely

32. *Three Generations.*
1918 approx. Wax crayon on paper.
68.6 × 45.7 cms
Ulster Folk Museum Collection.

ugly, we would at least have variety and something with which to contrast the beautiful.

But today it seems to me that tens of thousands of costumes – or whatever you call them – are turned out by the same machine in the same shape, the same colour and the same style; and tens of thousands of women will wear them, no matter whether they be gay, sad, thinkers, butterflies, old or young. The result will get the personality of one perhaps very indifferent dress-designer, who has no poetry or religion in her soul, duplicated tens of thousands of times.

I suppose clothes will answer me by saying, 'Well, I must be in fashion'. As if everyone of those girls has not something of her own self which is more beautiful than any uniform civilization could offer and why must we have a legion of newly painted dolls? Why must women be dominated by the personality of a dressmaker they do not even know?

Illustrating this, I use one of Conor's own stories.

When in America I had the pleasure to paint a number of beautiful society girls. One will always remain in my memory. To me she was a tragedy, though some thought her a miracle. She came to my studio in a faultless gown, not a stitch displaced; her hair was a wonderful undulation of waves; her colouring, off her dressing table, was without blemish – in fact, everything was perfect. She was famous as a beauty. I thought her a sheer mathematical creation. If only one little point in her had been imperfect – her hair slightly out of place – I think I could have worshipped her.

'I cannot indeed paint you like that,' I said. I told her why. Being Irish, I must have made some unintentionally funny remarks, for she laughed and laughed like a real human, and she became what she called untidy, and I called a 'real girl'.

'Just stay as you are,' I said, and I got my first sketch for the portrait.

She came next day as perfect as ever. Once again I tried to make her human – becoming almost a stage Irishman in the effort – but I failed. I am ashamed of my picture of her, although her friends thought it 'Poifectly divine'.

33. Early sketch.
8 March 1909. Pencil on paper.
21.6 × 13.5 cms
Linen Hall Library Collection, Belfast.

He held a rather romantic view of the shawl but certainly did not have a high opinion of hats:

Hats are, without doubt, one of modern civilisation's most dastardly crimes to women. They make almost every face alike. From a distance it is impossible to distinguish daughter from grandmother. That is why I want to see the return of the shawl. Of course, I do not mean necessarily a dull, ugly, woollen shawl.

There are countless materials – materials so light and diaphanous that they would be more of an aura to a beautiful head. But this is so very personal. There is no set way to wear it. Its lines keep hard or soft, sweeping or short, as the wearer wishes, and it can be arranged to suit personality and mood.

It is also very feminine. After all is it not in a sense one symbol of motherhood?

When not painting portraits I like to make crayon sketches of Ulster people in all their walks of life. I am exhibiting a few in town just now. It was while I was making these that I came across the Ulster mill-lassie in her shawl and realised that this was the headgear most suited to bring out beauty and personality. And these lassies realised it. They do not wear shawls out of necessity, but from choice. Even there, however, I fear the ugly talons of modern civilization have got their grip and girls are falling to the abominable cult of the cloche hat.

34. Detail from *Five studies of the Female Head 1908–1914*.
N.d. Pencil on paper.
19.1 × 14 cms
Linen Hall Library Collection, Belfast.

35. Early sketch.
N.d. Pencil on paper.
19 × 14.2 cms
Linen Hall Library Collection, Belfast.

36. *Girl with the Flaxen Hair*
(Dutchie Torney.)
N.d. Oil on plywood.
76.2 × 63.5 cms
George and Maura
McClelland Collection,
Dublin.

I want to protest in the strongest terms possible.
Girls were never more beautiful. But they must remember that womanhood is older than this present civilisation. They have a trust not to spoil that beauty which is their heritage.

R. Stephen Williams, the local correspondent of the *Daily Express*, reported in 1930 an interview with William Conor which took place in a 'populous bar somewhere on the outskirts of Belfast' and described the artist thus:

A man in an old and discoloured raincoat leans against the opposite wall surveying the scene. He is a man of medium height and powerful if ungainly build, thick set, rather short legged. A cloth cap, obviously unused to his head, is drawn down over a broad strongly marked face and eyes with a wealth of whimsical humour in them. A rather 'quare' face it is, too; a face with that unmistakable twist of fantasy in its contours; the face of a man who has seen fairies – and perhaps witches too – the face of a man whom those eternal devils

44

37. *Washing day.*
N.d. Oil.
50.8 × 61 cms
Arts Council of Northern
Ireland collection.

of intellectual unrest have driven forth in the infinite pursuit of beauty, in the unending effort to utter the unutterable. . . .

Like all really genuine artists, he is as interested in life as in art for he knows that the one cannot live without the other. . . .

The most awkward thing is his brogue (is 'brogue' the right word, I wonder?). It is a rich, furry explosive Northern Ireland accent, bewitching in its lilt and inflexion, but sometimes bafflingly hard to understand.

Beginning on 3 December 1930, Stephen Williams, under the title 'Beauty in Ulster', recorded interviews for the *Daily Express* with six subjects of portraits by Conor. Those chosen by the artist and whose portraits were reproduced in the paper were: Miss Dutchie Torney who had occasionally acted small parts with the Ulster Players, Mrs T. Walker, Lady Constance Malleson (*née* Annesley) – this was the Ulster actress, whose stage name was Collette O'Niel and who had studied at Sir Herbert Beerbohm Tree's school in London – Mrs Edgar Adams (*née* Blanche Bennett), Mrs Jack McCormic (*née* Jean Kay as she was known when she acted with the Ulster Players), and Miss Eleanor Honess.

# 7

# PUBLIC ACCLAIM, PRIVATE LOSS

During these years of exhibitions and the wider recognition of his work, Conor not only continued to produce pictures of his choice, but extended his range of subjects and sought commissions for portraits. He regarded portraiture as difficult, indeed he felt that only the artist quite understood how difficult. 'The job of a painter is not to make a map of a man's features but to represent the inner spirit.'

One of his more famous sitters was the first President of the Republic of Ireland, Dr Douglas Hyde. This occasion provided Conor with another but less dangerous experience of weapons, as reported in the *Irish Times*, in an article in August 1958.

> During one sitting the aged President fell into a doze, at a moment when the sun was coming through a window and casting a shadow on his face. Conor decided that one of the blinds in the room would have to be lowered but discovered that he could not reach it by hand. Taking down a gun which was hanging on a wall, he stood on a chair and made the necessary adjustment. As he stepped down again, an aide-de-camp suddenly entered the room, and was shocked to see the Ulster Presbyterian artist with a gun in his hand, which he appeared to be aiming at the President!

The picture now hangs in the Board Room of the Administration Building at University College, Dublin, where Dr Hyde was Professor of Modern Irish Language and Literature from 1909 to 1932.

Those who have seen the oil painting Conor made of his mother in 1919, could hardly disagree with the opinion of Richard Rowley and of many others who regarded this as his most outstanding portrait. The description of it from *The Irish Scene*, by Rowley, could hardly be surpassed.

48

The Painter has subdued all the details of the picture so as to throw into strong relief the nobly carved features, the white hair, the patient and steadfast eyes and the spiritualised loveliness of a face, marked with the passage of years, but still strong and full of courage.

This is to me a most satisfying portrait. The painting of the flesh tints is a triumph of delicacy; the modelling of forehead and nose and chin is powerful, and yet subdued to the natural frailness of the subject. But its chief charm consists not in its technical excellence but in its power to suggest the triumph of the spirit over old age and bodily decline.

One of his self-portraits, the painting *The Gombeen Man*, was hung at an Exhibition of the work of Living British Artists under the auspices of the British Artists' Exhibition opened at the Walker Art Gallery, Liverpool, on 26 March 1929. Catalogued as No. 48, the picture was priced at £50. This series of exhibitions, founded by Sir Joseph Duveen to publicise works by lesser-known artists and to help their sales, was first begun in 1927 and held at various galleries throughout Great Britain and Europe – Leeds, Paris, Brussels, Manchester, Bradford and Belfast, where Conor exhibited *At the Door* at £30. In 1928 the exhibitions were held in Plymouth, Buenos Aires, Venice and on board the Cunard liner *Berengaria*, during a voyage to and from New York; in 1929 they were held in Liverpool and Glasgow.

38. Dr Douglas Hyde sitting for his portrait.
Photograph from the Conor papers.
© *Irish Times*, Dublin.

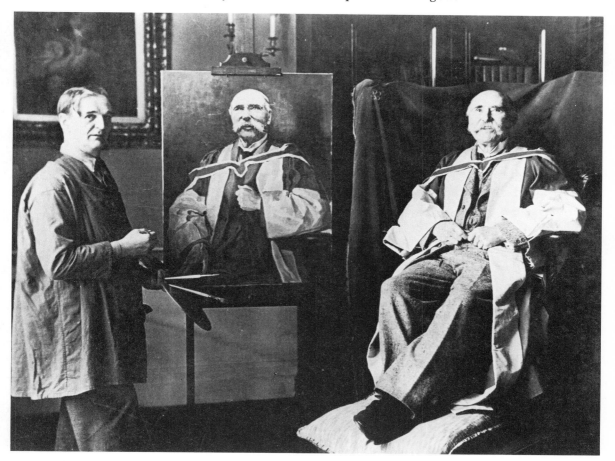

In October 1930 a large retrospective exhibition was arranged, by permission of the City of London Art Committee, in the City Guildhall. This was a loan collection of works sold during the past three years at the British Artists' Exhibitions. Mrs B. Edwards lent a watercolour picture by Conor, *Kelp Gatherers*, to this 'Living British Artists' Exhibition', which was opened by His Royal Highness Prince George.

In 1928, for the third time, Conor was elected as one of four Vice-Presidents of the Belfast Art Society, a position he held for one year. As a founder member he was elected one of the first nine Academicians when the Society became the Ulster Academy of Arts in 1930. He was also elected a foundation member of the National Society of Painters, Sculptors and Gravers, an organization which had been formed to bring together all the most important exponents of Modern Art. The Society was national in scope and included works by the most advanced modernists as well as by those adhering to the classical traditions. The first annual exhibition by the members, in painting, sculpture and

engraving, was held in the Grafton Galleries, London, and included four paintings by William Conor, *The Procession*, *Gospel Meeting*, *The Melodeon Player* and *Buying and Selling*.

Over the next two years he exhibited at the Society's Annual Exhibition a section of his design for *Ulster Past and Present*, on which he was then at work. This depicted a group of young Ulster workers coming towards the spectator, with gantries, towering cranes and linen factories in the background. He also showed *The Patchwork Quilt*, *The Cellist*, and a still life – an unusual subject matter for him – entitled *Daffodils*. When the Society exhibited during February 1932, this time in the Royal Institute Galleries, Piccadilly, London, three of the four Conor pictures shown were *The Jaunting Car*, *Youth and Age* and *The Market Women*.

It was in this year that he was invited by his friend Richard Rowley to design the costumes for *The Pageant of Saint Patrick* which Rowley had written to celebrate the 1500th anniversary of the Saint coming to Ireland. There were to be no fewer than 150 performers; Conor was assisted with the costumes by Lady Mabel Annesley. Conor also described, in the *Belfast Telegraph*, 12 April 1932, how he 'had spent many hours reading standard Irish works dealing with Tara's Hall and the early Kings of Ireland to enable him to form his ideas. He had also paid a special visit to Dublin to confer with Professor Macalister, the famous Irish archaeologist, whose advice had been particularly helpful... Barbaric design with brilliant colours to form the

41. A preliminary sketch of the costume design for Dichu, a character in Richard Rowley's *Pageant of St Patrick*, 1932.
Photograph from the Conor papers.

42. *Ulster Past and Present*. 1932. Oil on canvas. 205.7 × 749.3 cms
Ulster Museum Collection.
Photograph from the Conor papers.

background provide the basis of the costume scheme'. Conor also pointed out that history indicated that these were the ideas prevailing 1500 years ago. The first performance was held at Audley's Castle Strangford, and the second at Belfast Castle the following week, Saturday 18 June.

The warrior costumes designed for the Pageant were also shown in the large painting depicting *Ulster Past and Present*, unveiled at the Belfast Municipal Museum and Art Gallery by the Duke of Abercorn on 12 April. Later the picture was presented to the City and County Borough of Belfast by Sir Robert Baird, to whose influence Conor attributed his having received the commission. The City and County Borough in turn handed it over to the Museum for the benefit of the community. Sir Robert also purchased the cartoon for the original design and told Conor that he would like it presented to some institution. A draft letter written by Conor, dated 12 June 1934, to Sir Robert explained that he had been approached by the Governors of The Royal School, Armagh, who were anxious to have the cartoon. 'I thought that a historical school would be an ideal place to install the Fresco, and it is now being put up in the large hall, where it will be seen by many generations of young "Ulstermen". The Governors are putting a plaque upon the frame bearing the inscription "Presented to the School by Sir Robert Baird, K.B.E., D.L."'

The present Headmaster of the School, T.W. Mulryne, has informed me that the cartoon (oil on canvas) is still hanging in the Dining Hall

although it is his intention to move it to what he considers a more appropriate position in their new Library when it is completed.

*Ulster Past and Present* is a painting which began with a simple idea, an idea without any political meaning or statement, and which resulted in a very powerful and moving picture, totally truthful to the title.

It was one picture which filled Conor with satisfaction not only by his execution of it but by the public's response:

> ... words fail to express the elevation of my feelings since the Opening Ceremony. When I walk through town total strangers do come forward and shake my hand with such warmth, as to leave no doubt as to the sincerity of their congratulations. It is so gratifying to have inspired such feelings and I should be unnatural were I less vain at the present time.

Conor had also painted a portrait in oils of a former Headmaster of the Royal School, Armagh, Henry Hirsch. This picture was presented to Mr Hirsch by the old boys of the school on the occasion of his retirement in 1928.

Conor received further acclaim in 1932, when he became the first Irishman to be elected a Member of the Royal Institute of Oil Painters, entitling him to use after his name the Institute's Diploma letters, ROI; apparently this honour was generally considered to be only one step short of becoming a Royal Academician. A few months later in October he exhibited for the first time at the Institute's Annual Exhibition in their Piccadilly Galleries, London. Four of his pictures were shown and after the private viewing it was reported in an untitled newspaper review that 'a good many people were attracted by Mr. Conor's (*The Parade*), a parade of horses at an agricultural show. The animals are being led around the ring in single file, and the artist has drawn them with skill and understanding. The Council of the Institute have done Mr. Conor the honour of reproducing a photograph of his painting in their Catalogue.' His other works were *Point to Point*, *An Ulster Fair* and *Potato Gathering*, which was thought 'weak in draughtmanship and the figures are badly posed'. He did exhibit *The Orange Procession* at this year's Royal Academy but no work by him was hung again until 1935 (*Pedlars*); he did not become an RA.

John Hunter invited Conor to a preliminary meeting on 8 May 1933, called for the purpose of inaugurating a Guild of Artists. The invitation was also extended to Lady Mabel Annesley, Miss Kathleen M. Bridle, Miss Margaret and Miss Anne Yeames, Hugh E. Broderick, W. R. Gordon, Morris Harding, Edward L. Mansfield, Edward Marr, Padraig Marrinan, Colin Middleton and Romeo Toogood. These painters and sculptors gave themselves the title of 'The Northern Ireland Guild of Artists', and put on an Exhibition in the State Buildings, Arthur Square, Belfast, which also included works by John Luke. One of the pictures by Conor was of a coloured girl. When Miss Roberta Black, John Hewitt's fiancée, visited the exhibition she asked Conor why he was charging so much for his work, approximately £100, whilst everyone else was charging between £5 and £20. Conor was not pleased and said he had to think of his position as an artist. This also can be said of his pictures hanging in the Royal Hibernian Academy, Dublin, during the 1930s when few were more expensive than his.

The Guild petered out after this exhibition. When it was reformed in the following year, 1934, as the Ulster Unit, Broderick, Harding and Conor were no longer involved.

While sketching the working people of Belfast Conor was very aware of their surroundings and of their artistic talents, examples of which could be found on gable walls. On the 10 July 1933 the *Belfast Telegraph* published an article by Conor in which he commented on this art, at a time when the preparations for the Twelfth of July celebrations were almost complete:

> Whilst walking through the streets of our city during the week-end I was amazed at the amount of high artistic merit displayed on many of the mural decorations painted on various gables representing King William of Orange crossing the Boyne, the Siege of Derry and other important incidents of this historic period.
>
> It seems as if there is a revival of that very ancient art of decorating wall places, remains of which are being found in Egypt, India and Mexico, painted four or five thousand years before Christ. During the thirteenth century such outstanding craftsmen as Raphael and Leonardo da Vinci produced wonderful mural decorations, and in more recent times there were Puvis de Chauannes and Boucher in France, and today we have Frank Brangwyn and Gilbert Spencer in England. Perhaps it was from such humble beginnings as seen in Belfast that gave birth to these past masters in mural decoration.
>
> It is very creditable what these obscure humble painters have accomplished under great difficulties, since a certain rough wall surface of large dimensions has to be filled and the painter has to submit to the limitations set down by his cheap and rough and ready materials.
>
> I am fully aware that many of these paintings possess all the inevitable crudities of the amateur, and are gaudy in colour, smudged, and, on the whole, messy. But there are others that unquestionably show a certain affinity with primitive art, and those who produced them appear to have had in common with the primitives, who were men simply driven by the strong necessity of expressing what they feel, and having something to say, their one and only object is to say it, and that as completely and as deliberately as possible, leaving no doubt on the mind of the spectator as to the precise meaning of their expression.
>
> So, too, some of these wall decorations have been produced by men whose expression has not been impeded by a diligently studied technique of past generations nor has there been a cramping over difficult technicalities or art theories. They have set down or omitted nothing because of rule or precept, seem to know instinctively that the starting point lies beyond them in art and therein is found their chief appeal – their work is three parts instinctive.
>
> I know many people will say that these decorations are faulty in drawing because of a certain distortion and attenuation found in many of them but this only serves to give greater emphasis and strength to line and colour. Wrongly some people who dominate the intellectual life in Belfast frown on these paintings, but a great deal of this narrow-mindedness or indifference might be brushed aside if more sympathetic curiosity were aroused as to what these unknown and obscure painters are trying to do in our midst, and the manner in which they have given themselves up with enthusiasm to the embellishment of our city streets.

Sometime during 1931, the Connor family, who had lived for twenty-five years at No. 3 Landscape Terrace, Crumlin Road, removed to 62

43. *The Hillsborough Hunt.*
1950 approx. Oil on canvas.
61 × 50.8 cms
Ulster Folk Museum
Collection.

Westland Road, in a pleasant surburban area off the Antrim Road with a fine view of the Cave Hill. The house in Westland Road, for the short time the family lived there, was listed in the *Belfast Street Directory* in the name of William Conor. This was the only time in his life when a family home was in his name.

Here, after a long and tedious illness, his father died of a cerebral haemorrhage on 29 August 1933, at the age of 84. It is curious that this man, having lived to an advanced age and in the home of this now famous son, should have remained a very shadowy figure throughout what we know of Conor's life. I have not seen nor heard of any sketch of him being done, yet Conor remembered with pleasure some of the lovely metal work his father had left behind.

For William the death of his mother four months later, on 13 December, was a deeply felt emotional loss. Mary Connor died aged 81 of valvular disease of the heart. It is a measure of the depth of Conor's grief that, over the years, he continued to remark to friends that 'my only regret is that my mother did not live long enough to know of the recognition of my work'; in fact, he was well into his years of achievement at the time of her death. Certainly she was unable to share with him the honours of the Associate Membership the Royal Hibernian Academy in 1938, Full Membership in 1946, the OBE in 1952, an Honorary MA of Queen's University, Belfast in 1957, the Presidency of the Royal Ulster Academy in 1957 and the Civil List Award in 1959.

Although not a member of the New English Art Club, Conor exhibited two works at their eighty-fourth annual exhibition at their Suffolk Street Galleries, London, which opened on 19 October 1933. His two oils were No. 369 *Market Day* and No. 374 *The House Fair*.

When the Government of the Irish Free State decided to participate

56

officially in the Chicago Century of Progress, an exhibition which ran from June to November, 1933, a small committee was set up to ensure that there would be a representative display of pictures by living Irish artists. Conor was invited to submit two or three examples of his work which he considered suitable for the exhibition. These were to be sent to the School of Art, Kildare Street, Dublin, for a final selection to be made with the assistance of a representative of the Department of Industry and Commerce before being shipped to Chicago. Unfortunately it had not been made sufficiently clear that the pictures were to be of Free State interest so neither of his two works was included. His *Orange Procession* was not, in the opinion of the Minister's representative, of Free State interest, nor was *Ship-Builders*, as the small flag in the centre might have been taken to represent a Union Jack.

In October 1934 Conor was again receiving favourable reviews for the great versatility in the subject matter of the four pictures hung at the Royal Institute of Oil Painters. The titles were *Exercising Greyhounds*, *Start of the 25 yards Race* (a study of a young girls' swimming race), *Coming from the Well* and *The Meet of County Down Staghounds, Hillsborough*, in which

> . . . we see his power to infuse individuality into his painting. We have a view of the main street in Hillsborough, with its rising hills beyond. In the foreground are a number of huntsmen and huntswomen and hounds waiting to move off, all bathed in brilliant sunshine. . .

The Thomas Haverty Trust was founded by Thomas Haverty, Dublin, to purchase every year works of high order or merit by Irish artists throughout Ireland and to present or lend them to various Art Galleries and Public Buildings, in both the North and the South. The Trust purchased a set of sixteen pastel costume designs of Irish historical figures for the Saint Patrick's Pageant and presented them to the Hugh Lane Gallery, Dublin, in 1935. They also purchased *The Jaunting Car* which had been exhibited at the 1933 Royal Hibernian Academy, and in 1936 presented it to the Belfast Municipal Museum and Art Gallery.

Conor's work was becoming more widely known and the following letter by him, 'An Artist's Warning', which appeared in the *Belfast Telegraph*, 15 March 1935, is of considerable interest and importance:

> Sir, – My attention has been drawn to one or two instances where some person or persons have made paintings in imitation of my work, and signed these with a clever imitation of my signature. I have examined some of these paintings, which were shown to me by a dealer, and find that the paintings and signature are spurious. I think the public should be informed of the matter, and advised to have any pictures produced as my work, and which they propose buying, examined by an expert. At present I am taking legal action on the matter with the object of tracing the bogus paintings to their source.

In mid-June 1935 the completed portrait of the Most Reverend Dr Charles F. D'Arcy, Archbishop of Armagh and Primate of all Ireland, went on view at the Belfast and Municipal Art Gallery, before joining the collection of old paintings at The Palace, Armagh. A further fifteen St Patrick's Pageant costume designs, including those for the main characters, were purchased for £50 by Archbishop D'Arcy and

44. *College Hill Armagh.*
N.d. Oil.
45.7 × 33 cms
Arts Council of Northern
Ireland Collection.

presented by him to hang in Church House, Armagh. An extract from the Minutes of a special meeting of the Diocesan Council held on 8 October 1935 records the gift. 'Proposed by the Earl of Belmore, Seconded by Reverend T. J. McEndoo and passed: "That the best thanks of the Council be given to the Primate, and Congratulations to the Artist for the Pictures in the Council Room".'

During the previous year, while Conor was in Armagh, he made a conté crayon study in black and red of his friend the artist George MacCann. It was a study Conor thought very effective and one of his most successful.

When George MacCann married Mercy Hunter in 1935, Conor gave the picture to them as a wedding present.

Bradford Corporation invited Conor in April 1936 to lend them his painting *The Pedlars*, which had been hung on the line at the Royal Academy the previous year. As the painting had been sold at the Academy he was unable to accede to the request, but sent them another painting of Ulster country life, *Youth and Age*, an old woman and a girl coming from their work in the fields.

Considered to be an interesting development in the art world was the Circulating Exhibition by the Art Exhibition Bureau, London, in which Conor was also represented. The idea behind the Exhibition was that art-lovers in every part of the United Kingdom should be given an opportunity to see the best work shown in various London Galleries during Jubilee year (1935). With that object in view, the Bureau selected one hundred paintings by contemporary modern British painters which they felt to be typical of all that was vital and interesting in the work of that year.

The Conor painting selected was one entitled *My Brother*. When it had been hung the previous year at the Royal Society of Portrait Painters' Exhibition in London, the strong and forceful treatment had

58

attracted the attention of some of the leading London critics.

During 1936 Conor, back in London for a short stay at the Chelsea Arts Club, was commissioned by friends of Alderman Denys Lowson to paint his portrait as a wedding present; he was to be married to the Honourable Patricia MacPherson, daughter of Lord and Lady Strathcarron, ten days later, on 17 July. Sittings for the portrait were given at Denys Lowson's city office; he afterwards gave Conor a pocket watch as a mark of appreciation. Alderman Lowson later became Lord Mayor of London for the year 1950–51.

A further recognition was bestowed upon Conor on 16 November 1936 when he was made an Honorary Academician of the Ulster Academy of the Arts.

In 1937 came further domestic change when Conor, with his sister Mary, and his brothers John, Martin and Russell, moved from 62 Westland Road to 107 Salisbury Avenue, Belfast, which was at the end of a row of double-fronted terrace houses. It was rented in the name of Russell Connor, who was at that time still employed in the Northern Ireland Postal Service. This was to be William Conor's home for the remainder of his life.

Through the kindness of Paul Henry, Conor received information about two of his earlier pictures. In a letter delivered by Henry, dated 3 July, 1937, he learned from James A. Healy of New York, that he had purchased at auction a picture by Conor entitled *Market Women*, which bore on the back the label of the Godfrey Phillips Gallery, London. Healy also reported that he had rescued, again from auction, a pastel portrait which Conor had made, during his stay in New York in 1926, of the now late Judge Dick Campbell and of its now hanging on the 'Richard Campbell Memorial Panel', on the walls of the American Irish Historical Society. Apparently a group, which had included James Healy who knew of Judge Campbell's interest in the Society, had arranged for this portrait to be hung in the Society's Library as a tribute to his memory; the formal presentation was made on 7 May 1936. Although Judge Campbell had a great interest in art, this picture by William Conor appears to be the only portrait of him, photographic or otherwise. The portrait now hangs in the Society's present premises at 991 Fifth Avenue; the Librarian and Archivist, William D. Griffin, who kindly sent me a copy of their magazine illustrating this portrait, informed me that 'it was done in shades of red'.

From studies made at a Garden Party at Stormont on the 28 July 1937, Conor painted a portrait of His Majesty King George VI, and presented it to the Ulster Branch of the Overseas League to hang in the Ulster Room at Overseas House, London. In the same year he exhibited again at the Royal Academy, London. Their acceptance of his picture *Strangford Lough, Co. Down* pleased him greatly, as it was 'my first big landscape'.

A close friend of Conor's was Leslie Montgomery, a bank manager who had been born in Downpatrick, Co Down, and who wrote under the pseudonym of Lynn C. Doyle, a name which had suggested itself to him from an item on an invoice – Linseed Oil. He later dropped the 'C'. Publishing *Ballygullion*, his first volume of humorous stories, when a bank clerk in Dublin in 1908, Lynn Doyle later became known as a lecturer, broadcaster and literary critic; it was he who opened, on 21 April 1938, Conor's exhibition at Combridge's Gallery, Grafton Street, Dublin. Nearly all the subjects depicted peasant and working life in the West of Ireland and included an oil *Coming from Mass* and a watercolour *On the River near Ballynahinch, Connemara*.

From Conor's equally close friend, R. V. Williams (pen-name Richard Rowley), came a fine tribute to the quality of the artist's landscape work. This was in a letter written to Leslie Montgomery on 18 February 1937, and is a sympathetic yet incisive appreciation of Conor's ability in this genre.

> He has been painting a lot of landscapes in oil and some of them are quite exquisite. He has about 20 done now, and I find them very impressive, They are very freely handled, and have a very rich paint-quality; their colour seems to me charming, and all of them have a sense of design which is sometimes absent

46. A photograph taken in 1926 of, 1–r; Conor, Leslie Montgomery (Lynn Doyle) and R. V. Williams (Richard Rowley) after the Belfast Rotarian luncheon at which Leslie Montgomery was the guest speaker.
Photograph from the Conor Papers.
*Belfast News Letter*, 27 January 1926.

from his figure work. Although they are definitely modern in their handling and in their insistence on pattern, yet he manages, without being sentimental, to infuse them with a subtly romantic feeling, which, I must admit, appeals to me. It is as if Willie said to himself as he painted 'This bit of landscape gave me delight, and I'm not a bit ashamed to show how much it moves me'. If he can do another twenty as good as these, he'll have a show worth looking at. The least successful thing he has done so far is worth the whole of Paul's exhibition which we saw when I was in Dublin – in fact there's been no one in Ireland since Nathaniel Hone, who could produce a collection of landscapes so rich, so varied, and so original. When I saw what he had done and put them all up in the studio together, I was astonished and delighted. I really had no idea that Willie would prove himself so *great* a painter of landscape. If you're in Dublin you ought to call in Combridge's and tell them what you have heard about Conor's landscapes. They ought to make a sensation. Combridge's should jump at the chance of showing them.

In October 1938, after having exhibited many times there, William Conor was elected an Associate of the Royal Hibernian Academy, Dublin, although he lived too far away to be able to act as an officer or to teach in the School of the Academy. They were rather anxious that Members should be able to attend meetings and help with the work but the position did enable him to send eight pictures each year without the worry of their being turned down. It was not until 1946 that he was elected a full member of the Academy.

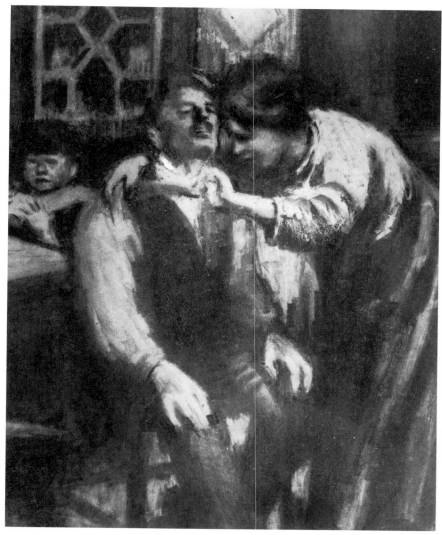

It is difficult to understand why Conor was not recognised earlier by the RHA. He had, after all, exhibited there for the first time in 1918, when six of his works were hung. Between 1918 and 1938, when he was made an Associate Member, he had exhibited at twelve of the Annual Exhibitions and had become a known and respected artist both in and outside his native Province, meriting very favourable reviews in Great Britain, France and America. Between 1938 and 1946, when he was made a Full Member of the RHA, he exhibited in each of the eight years. He was then sixty-five years of age.

47. *Two Shawlies.*
N.d. Watercolour on paper.
29.2 × 22.9 cms
George and Maura
McClelland collection,
Dublin.

Three other painters from the North of Ireland, who received recognition at a younger age than Conor, were James Humbert Craig (1878–1944), who was made an Associate in 1925 and Full Member in 1928, Paul Henry (1877–1958), an Associate in 1926 and Full Member in 1929, and Frank McKelvey (1895–1974), an Associate in 1923 and a Full Member in 1930.

Was it that these three artists were producing work, mainly landscape, that was more readily acceptable to and appreciated by the Southern public than Conor's work with its more individual style of drawing and painting? His subjects were mainly representative of ordinary Northern folk and the work of their everyday lives and reflected a highly industrialised society.

The International Business Machines Corporation (IBM) approached the Belfast Municipal Museum and Art Gallery requesting them to suggest two artists, an established artist and an up-and-coming one, to submit pictures for their display of 'The Art of 79 Countries', at the New York World's Fair in 1939. The Curator, Arthur Deane, put forward the names of William Conor, who happened to be a close friend, and John Luke. Eventually the Corporation acquired Conor's *Irish Horse Parade* and Luke's *Slievemore* to represent Northern Ireland. The Corporation presented to Conor and all artists who contributed work an inscribed medallion as an Honorary Award for a notable contribution to the art of the World. The exhibition subsequently toured art centres in America and the other countries.

Despite Conor's continuing achievements and increasing recognition he still derived interest and pleasure from his early habit of rapid sketches when his subjects were unaware. There were times when his caution was amusingly unsuccessful. On one occasion he was sketching in Alexander Park off the Antrim Road, Belfast. He saw two little girls, whom he found interesting, sitting on one of the long bench seats and thought, 'Well I'll slip on to the other end and make notes of them in my usual method'. But he was very much surprised to hear one of them say, 'Say, Maggie – look at this aul cod, he's making sketches of us and he thinks we don't know'. He, of course, slipped away after that.

To me such an incident reflects his sense of humour; this, with his deep love of the Belfast people, comes across very vividly in his pictures. To know the Ulster dialect is all one needs for these pictures to come truly alive and for the sense of local identity to be complete. Yet it should be remembered that he never thought of himself as a propagandist or a man with a message.

> It is not my job to draw deductions or preach sermons on social subjects, all my life my aim has been to seek for beauty in those places where it is not often sought, in crowded thoroughfares, in the factory and in the shipyard.

# 8

# WAR ARTIST AGAIN

With the outbreak of the Second World War in 1939, Conor was again asked to make sketches of Ulster's War Effort. In April 1940, he received a letter from the Ministry of Information, London, on behalf of the Artists' Advisory Committee, who had been especially interested in the figure subjects in colour which Conor had sent to them. The Committee had recommended that he be commissioned to undertake a series of six or eight drawings illustrating Ulster's contribution to the war effort, such as work in the shipyards and the training of troops. For his work he was offered a fee of £50, with travelling expenses and maintenance allowance at a flat rate of £1 a day, should he be required to be away from home to study the subject at first hand. All the work done in connection with this Commission was vested solely in the Crown; even his friends were not permitted to view the work before it had been submitted to the Ministry for censorship.

In this same month, he again exhibited at Combridges Gallery, Dublin. *Girl from the West, Mother and Child, Open Air Market* and *The Blind Fiddler* were among those which were on view.

The Ministry of Information wrote to Conor advising him that they were opening a third gallery to the public in the War Artists' Exhibition at the National Gallery, London, on 26 August 1940, and that his picture, *Building an Air Raid shelter in a Belfast Street*, was to be exhibited.

A special exhibition consisting of the work commissioned by the Ministry from Conor was regarded as one of the features of Belfast's War Weapons Week when it opened on 2 December 1940, in the Ulster Arcade (Brands) Ltd. The exhibition was visited by the Duke of

49. Conor's exhibition held at the Ulster Arcade (Brands) Ltd.
L–r; M. G. Martin (Manager), Moore Brand (Managing Director), Conor and the Lord Mayor, Sir Crawford McCullagh. All the pictures being viewed are now in the Ulster Museum collection. The seven pictures clearly seen are:-
Top row, l–r; *Grenade Throwing Practice, Looking at Aeroplanes, F.A.N.Y's crossing Donegall Place, Belfast.*
Middle row, l–r; *Men Working at a Shelter, Soldier on Point Duty, Study for Grenade Throwing Practice.*
Bottom row; *Men of the Home Front.*
*Belfast Telegraph*, 3 December 1940.

Abercorn, then Governor of Northern Ireland, the Prime Minister Sir Basil Brooke and the Lord Chief Justice. The next day the Lord Mayor, Sir Crawford McCullough, paid an official visit. It would seem that those works which did not sell were among the war drawings which the Municipal Museum and Art Gallery purchased from Conor the following year. The final total of monies raised by Belfast's War Weapons Week was announced on 10 December 1940: it had reached the amazing total of £6,784,889, or the equivalent of £5 6s 0d per head of the population of Northern Ireland.

During the period leading up to the second Blitz on Belfast in May 1941, William, John, Russell, Martin (now returned from America) and Mary went to stay for some months with their three cousins the Misses Milliken in Carryduff. (The parents were now dead and the two elder brothers had left Northern Ireland many years before, Matthew to England in 1912, with his wife and year old son Wallace, and Hugh to Canada in 1909, with his wife Edith.) This stay had its difficulties as the Connors were not particularly religious and the Millikens were, as can be appreciated by a story which Conor related to James Vitty:

One night as we were going back to bed after the 'all clear' had sounded, we heard the air-raid sirens a second time so we again took shelter only to find later that it was one of the Miss Millikens singing psalms on her way upstairs to bed.

While staying with his cousins Conor had to be on his best behaviour

66

and watch what he said. When it came to mealtimes, he was greatly embarrassed as he was often asked to say Grace and could never think of a proper Grace to say. A brother, the late Matthew Milliken, who had then lived close by, told me how the Connors would accompany him each morning when he took his three children to school in Belfast. In the evenings as there was nothing much to do they would amuse themselves with the children. Conor would make sketches of them on scraps of paper which they would think lovely, 'as like them to a tee' but he would tear them up, thinking them not good enough. However he was to make up for this in later years on the occasions of marriages in this family, when he gave his pictures as wedding presents.

A draft letter by Conor dated 19 May 1941, to Robert Gransden, the Secretary to the Cabinet, Stormont, Belfast, reads:

> Sometime ago I was commissioned by the Ministry of Information to do some drawings illustrative of the War Effort of Northern Ireland, and my drawings have been exhibited by the Ministry in England, Scotland and in the United States. It has been a gratification to me that I have been permitted by the War Artists Committee to show a wide audience the great deeds that have been performed by my fellow countrymen in the cause of Freedom.
>
> It has recently occurred to me that so many Ulstermen are found in Command of the King's armies that a series of portraits of Ulster Generals would make a unique record of the Military prowess of our Province, and if hung at Stormont would make a permanent memorial of Ulster's contribution to the present war. The names that suggest themselves to me are: General Sir John Dill, Lieutenant General Sir Allen [sic] Brooke, Lieutenant General H. G. Alexander, Air Marshall Tyrell, General McCarrison, Wing Commander F. V. Beamish but no doubt others could be added.

50. *F.A.N.Y's Crossing Donegall Place, Belfast.* 1940. Crayon on paper. 47.8 × 29 cms Ulster Museum Collection, Belfast.

51. *Collecting Scrap Metal.* 1940. Crayon on paper. 34.7 × 44.5 cms sight Ulster Museum Collection, Belfast.

If you think this suggestion would interest the P.M. and the Members of the Cabinet, I should be very happy to call and discuss the project with you.

Interest was displayed when Gransden wrote on 5 June to Sir Wilfred Spender, the Permanent Secretary, Department of Finance, about Conor's suggestion. Sir Wilfred, after consulting the Minister of Finance, Milne Barbour, agreed with Gransden's doubt 'whether public funds could be used in the way suggested'. On being informed of this, Conor wrote on 1 July, asking for a private interview with Gransden. As a result of this interview Gransden again wrote to Sir Wilfred Spender on 10 July, stating the idea now proposed by Conor, that a number of Ulster artists be employed to depict Ulster's War Effort, with himself being engaged on portrait work. Sir Wilfred, writing on 15 July, again squashed the idea after consultation with Barbour. The following day Sir Wilfred communicated this decision to Conor.

However, the idea of Conor doing something was not dropped immediately. On 24 September Mrs Dehra Parker, the Parliamentary Secretary of the Ministry of Education, wrote to the Prime Minister, J. M. Andrews, pressing the necessity for 'some tangible pictorial record of Ulster work done during this war', and nominating Conor as the most suitable man to undertake such work. As a result of this the Prime Minister agreed to inspect some of Conor's work – one in particular, *Collecting Scrap Metal*, is mentioned in a note from Gransden to Mrs Parker on 6 November – but again it was decided not to engage Conor, nor to purchase any of his pictures. For some reason Gransden did not write to Conor to inform him of this decision until 29 July 1942, although Mrs Parker had already done so in a private capacity.

The *Bell* magazine in July 1941 reported that people in all the Arts had 'combined to create a Fund in affectionate memory of Fred Higgins' (the poet F. R. Higgins, who had died that year). Conor was one of eighteen painters who each generously donated a picture for a Prize Drawing on 4 October, blocks of tickets for which could be had by application to Lynn Doyle at 4 Clare Street, Dublin.

In the Linen Salon of Robinson and Cleaver's, on 6 August 1941, the Duchess of Abercorn opened an exhibition by William Conor entitled 'Air Raid Memories', illustrating Blitz scenes in Belfast during the previous three months. The Duchess, when asked by Conor to choose a benevolent fund to receive twenty per cent of the proceeds, nominated the Royal Air Force Benevolent Fund.

One of his coloured drawings, *Arnott's after Air Raid 1941*, was purchased seventeen years later by John Arnott and Company (Belfast) Ltd, for £25 5s 0d.

In 1943 Conor received a letter from the Headquarters, European Theatre of Operations, United States Army, enquiring if it were true that he had painted a picture of the original landing of the American troops in Northern Ireland on 26 January 1942, and if so, what had become of the picture, as it was possible that the United States Army might wish to purchase it.

The picture referred to was a 24″ × 19″ colour drawing in crayon;

52. *Thornton's and Lindsay's,*
*Donegall Place, Belfast,*
*Morning After Air Raid.*
1941. Crayon on paper.
45.7 × 35.6 cms
Linen Hall Library Collection,
Belfast.

53. *Tramway Depot after Air*
*Raid, Belfast.*
1941. Crayon on paper.
44 × 33.7 cms sight
Ulster Museum Collection,
Belfast.
Donated in 1947 by War
Artist's Advisory Committee,
through Imperial War
Museum, London.

54. *A Roof Spotter*.
1940. Crayon on paper.
45.5 × 35.4 cms
Ulster Museum Collection,
Belfast.

William Conor was the only artist to be given a permit to make a drawing of the historic occasion. As well as this, he also made a collection of drawings of about eighteen subjects of American military life in Northern Ireland. Although Conor sent the American Army a black and white photograph of the drawing and intimated he would make a larger picture of it if they wished, the American Army Historical Services Division recently advised me that they could find no record of having purchased such a picture. Among those included in the drawing are Major-General Russel P. Hartle, Commanding United States Troops, who has already disembarked from the ship, His Grace the Duke of Abercorn Governor of Northern Ireland, and Sir Archibald Sinclair, British Air Minister, greeting Private Milburn Henke, the first American soldier officially to step on British soil, with the Band of the Royal Ulster Rifles playing in the background.

James Vitty remembers Conor telling him about an incident in the

55. *Evacuation of Children,
Great Northern Railway
Station, Belfast.*
1940 approx. Pencil and wax
crayon on paper.
34.5 × 46 cms
Ulster Museum Collection,
Belfast.
Donated in 1947 by War
Advisory Committee through
Imperial War Museum,
London.

early years of the war. He was going up in the lift to his studio in 1 Wellington Place, when a stockbroker looked at him in surprise and said, 'I thought, Mr Conor, that you in a profession like yours would have joined up by now'. Willie said, 'There I was standing looking on myself as a bastion of civilization and this jumped-up bookie was suggesting I should go to war instead of him.'

Another story was related to William Carter. After an air raid on Belfast, Conor obtained permission from Leahy, Kelly & Leahy, then on the corner of Castle Place, to work from their upstairs stores making sketches of the bomb damage to High Street, but for some reason someone thought he was spying. These stories emphasise, in William Carter's opinion, that he didn't think William Conor had enjoyed the work in the Second World War as he was mostly recording the dismal scenes of damage and destruction instead of being able to follow the natural creative work of an artist. He may however have gained some interest in recording the reactions of people towards the air raids and the evacuation of families and children from Belfast.

The work he did then was not, I think, of any great significance in his life as an artist. I think he hated the war and he hated everything to do with it. Of course economically it was a difficult time, the wartime interfered with normal work and normal activities and the fact that he couldn't travel easily outside the Province. I think it was a bad period of his life that he didn't like to remember or talk about.

56. 11A Stranmillis Road.
Conor's studio from 1944–1959.

57. *Landing of the First
American Troops in Northern
Ireland.*
26 January 1942. Crayon on
paper.
48.3 × 61 cms sight
Linen Hall Library Collection,
Belfast.

He had left his studio at Wellington Place in 1940, thereafter giving his address either as Salisbury Avenue or the nearby Academy Club at 18 Brookhill Avenue. He did not acquire another studio until 1944 when he moved into 11a Stranmillis Road, a neat single storey building in a terrace of three storey houses sited directly across the road from the Belfast Municipal Museum and Art Gallery, which is pleasantly situated in grounds which are bounded by the Botanical Gardens on one side and by the old and historic Friar's Bush graveyard on the other. It was a quiet and congenial area.

# 9

# MAINLY OF BOOKS
# AND
# BOOKMEN

William Conor's book, *The Irish Scene*, was published by Derrick MacCord, Belfast, in 1944. The foreword was by E. M. O'R. Dickey, MA, himself a painter and wood engraver of landscapes; a critical appreciation was written by Richard Rowley. The book comprised twelve plates of Conor's work, six in colour and the rest in monochrome. The publisher's leaflet noted:

> His coloured crayon drawings are prized and sought for by collectors who appreciate strength of design, richness of tone and a masterful draughtmanship that never degenerates into a mere technical swagger. The Publisher hopes that this survey of Conor's work will meet with the favour of the public. It forms a modest and yet sincere tribute to the artistic labours of a fine painter.

A draft letter by Conor amongst his papers, dated 30 December 1946, records the unfortunate news that the publishers had gone bankrupt and although 'close on a thousand copies' had been sold he 'never received any royalties'.

Thirty pictures by William Conor were shown at the CEMA exhibition of 1945–46 held in Tyrone House, Belfast, before being the first of a series of one man shows to tour the Province – Enniskillen, Londonderry, Magherafelt, Larne, Portadown, Ballycastle and again in Belfast in the foyer of the Assembly Hall during the Musical Festival. Among Conor's work shown were *The Girl with the Flaxen Hair* (Dutchie Torney), *Strangford Lough*, *Ardglass Fisher Girls*, *Winter on the River Lagan* and *Market Day*.

In 1946 he painted a number of portraits, one of which was that of his

58. Conor working at his
portrait of St John Ervine.
1946. Photograph from the
Conor Papers.
The portrait is now in the
Ulster Museum Collection,
Belfast.

friend St John Ervine. Ervine was born in Belfast in 1883, became a
playwright, critic, novelist and a Member of the Irish Academy of
Letters. He moved to Dublin in 1915, where for a short time he was
Manager of the Abbey Theatre. He later moved to England, living in
Seaton, Devon. Conor's portrait he thought 'a brilliant piece and I am
proud to be its owner'. Although Ervine's wife regarded the painting as
being good she felt that Conor did not see him as she did:

> I think if I was walking through an art gallery I'd stop and say, 'Isn't that man
> like St. John' but I'd never say 'that's St. John'. The mouth I do not recognise
> at all and the face seems a little too broad or not long enough and there is a
> weakness that is not the real St. John and he looks so much older and feeble
> than he does in reality. Still I'm sure it is a fine painting but alas! you just
> haven't caught the St. John I know.
> Sir Edward Mellanby a friend who knows him well feels much as I do.

74

St John Ervine was later to express to Conor how glad he was to hear that Robert Lynd, essayist and critic, was to sit for him in September. Lynd, born in Belfast in 1879, later moved to London and for many years was Literary Editor of the *News Chronicle* and also contributed to the *New Statesman*, signing himself 'Y.Y.' The Lynd portrait is now in the collection of the Linen Hall Library, Belfast.

Conor also made a portrait in crayon on paper of another local friend, Thomas Carnduff, the shipyard worker, poet and playwright, whose plays were presented by Richard Hayward and the Belfast Repertory Theatre Company. The combination of local theatre, poetry, novels, plays and Conor's paintings and drawings provided what John Hewitt has aptly described as the 'Urban Phase, the breakthrough in Urban Belfast', covering the period from early Twenties to the early Thirties. This surge of creativity was possibly a reaction to the 1914–18 War (which Thomas Carnduff had experienced in France with the Royal Engineers), the tragically high losses of local men and the increasingly painful realities of the post-war period and the Depression.

The Conor drawing of Carnduff was originally commissioned by Richard Rowley and intended to be included in one of a series of books on writers who contributed to his Mourne Press publications. The idea behind the Mourne Press, which was formed in 1940, was to provide books of a good quality at a modest price which would be available in local as well as in city bookshops. Rowley was not only editor but salesman, business-manager, invoice clerk and book-keeper; the printing was done at the press of the *Banbridge Chronicle*. His press failed due to disappointing sales and constant paper shortages; he himself fell seriously ill during 1941. Of the sixteen titles originally announced only six were published. Although Conor had made the portrait, Carnduff's book was not among the six. However all the portraits commissioned from various artists were given by Rowley to the Municipal Museum and Art Gallery, Belfast.

Apart from Richard Rowley dedicating his book *The Piper of Mourne and other poems* to Conor, he made use of an incident which had happened to the artist (Michael Williams, Rowley's son, believes that it took place when Conor and his father were on holiday in the Isle of Man) and adapted this into a story entitled 'The Douai Version' which appeared in *Northern Harvest: An Anthology of Ulster Writing*; both books were published by Derrick MacCord in 1944. The story also appeared in *Brave Crack*, an anthology of wit and humour published by H. R. Carter, Belfast, in 1950. Conor's two lino cuts *The Connoisseur* and *The Peacemaker* were included in the cartoon section of the book.

Richard Rowley's death in 1947 ended a long and close friendship. It had brought to Conor the warm quality of family life when he visited the Williamses at their home at Brook Cottage, Newcastle, where he made sketches of the children during the 1920s. Richard Rowley, the pen name of Richard Valentine Williams, was not only a prolific poet, author of short stories and verse-plays, but a handkerchief manufac-turer with the family firm of McBride and Williams, 19 Ormeau Avenue, Belfast, until it fell a victim to the economic depression in 1932. It was reconstituted the following year, but with Rowley only a nominal

59. *Thomas Carnduff*
(1886–1956).
1943 approx. Crayon on paper.
38.3 × 28 cms
Ulster Museum Collection,
Belfast.

60. *Mother and Child.*
N.d. Oil and wax crayon on
canvas textured board.
76.2 × 55.9 cms
George and Maura
McClelland Collection,
Dublin.

Director. At one time either to advertise or illustrate the gift boxes for their 'Ormo' handkerchiefs the company had made use of a coloured drawing which Conor had produced depicting a young man and woman leaning on the top of a wall. Similar versions of this drawing, entitled *Weavers*, are in the care of the Ulster Museum and the Ulster Folk and Transport Museum.

For the opening in 1947 of the Government of Northern Ireland's new offices in London, CEMA were asked to present an exhibition of Ulster painters; included were William Conor who showed five works, Rowel Friers, John Hunter, John Luke, Frank McKelvey, Colin Middleton and Sidney Smith. Sadly, it seems that the exhibition attracted very little public attention.

In the same year a Canadian firm, Messrs Cook of Toronto, produced a brochure and advertising cards for a promotional scheme using five crayon drawings which had been purchased in May 1946, from Conor on their behalf, by the Raceview Woollen Mills, Ballymena.

76

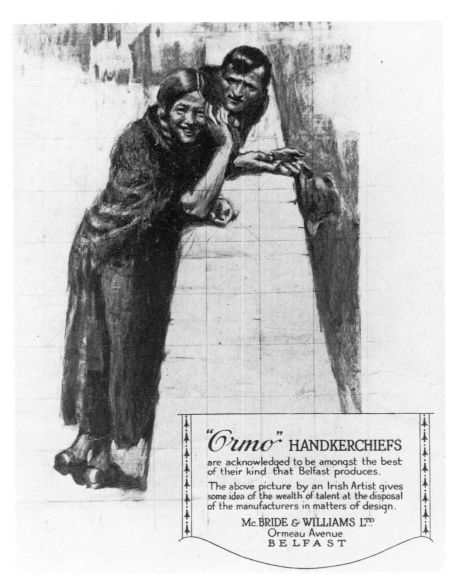

"Ormo" HANDKERCHIEFS

are acknowledged to be amongst the best
of their kind that Belfast produces.

The above picture by an Irish Artist gives
some idea of the wealth of talent at the disposal
of the manufacturers in matters of design.

Mc.BRIDE & WILLIAMS L<sup>TD</sup>
Ormeau Avenue
BELFAST

61. *Weavers.*
This was used either for
advertising or to illustrate
the gift boxes of 'Ormo'
handkerchiefs for McBride
and Williams Ltd., pre 1932.
Illustration from the Conor
papers.

Michael Sheill and Son (Grocer and Provision Merchants, Bagenalstown, County Carlow) commissioned Conor in 1948 to make from a
passport size snapshot, a black and white drawing of the late Daniel
McGrath. They agreed with Conor's suggestion that the portrait should
be life size. The snapshot proved to be very small and with little detail,
but when he had finished the head-and-shoulders portrait in black conté
crayon, it was regarded by those concerned that under the circumstances it was a very good likeness and a forceful drawing. Unfortunately Conor failed to return the snapshot but I have been told by
John Sheill that the portrait is now hanging in the McGrath Hall,
Bagenalstown.

Mr Sheill also explained that Daniel McGrath had been born in
Bagenalstown and trained in a tea firm; later, with his two brothers, he

set up a tea business in 3 Batchelor Walk, Dublin. He never married and when he died in 1943, he willed three-quarters of the residue of his estate to the people of Bagenalstown to build a hall and sportsfield and £25 to be given to each poor girl on the morning of her marriage.

On 15 April 1948 an exhibition of Conor's work was held in the Victor Waddington Galleries, Dublin. The following day a review of the exhibition in the *Irish Times* not only mentioned pictures such as *The Girl with the Cart*, *Taking the Last Jump*, *Coal Buckets*, *The Hand Bellows* and the landscape *Bog and Meadow*, but continued:

> No matter what be an artist's intention all remains a dream unless he has the technique to express it, and Conor has a very rich technique, not only is his drawing massive and solid, his colour rich and varied but he has that mysterious quality called 'touch'.

In October 1950 CEMA held a Conor exhibition in their Donegall Place Gallery, Belfast, for which John Hewitt wrote a sonnet as a foreword to the catalogue. The exhibition, which was opened by Lynn Doyle, was slightly marred – or perhaps enlivened – by the versatile if rather eccentric local artist and sculptor John Langtry Lynas who, objecting to Doyle's high opinion of Conor, left the exhibition thumping his stick and shouting 'balderdash'. Among the sixteen oil paintings exhibited were *Flax Gatherers*, *Standing Room Only*, *Listening to the Band*, *The Accordion Player* and *The Path through the Woods*; the nine crayon drawings included *The Sulky Child*, *Step Together*, *Queueing in the Rain*, *Chair-o-Planes*, *The Point to Point* and *By Winding Roads*; three watercolours were *Scrabo*, *Still Waters* and *The Rustle of Spring*.

The portrait of the late Lord Farnham, which was exhibited at a retrospective exhibition by CEMA in the Museum and Art Gallery, Belfast, in 1957, was painted expressly for the Grand Masonic Lodge of Ireland by Conor in 1950. The picture is now hanging in Freemasons' Hall, Dublin. This portrait was accepted and hung at the RHA Annual Exhibition in 1951, but was so positioned as not to be seen to any advantage because of reflections on the glass.

The Festival of Britain was opened by King George VI on 3 May 1951; Conor received an invitation to a Service of Dedication in St. Paul's Cathedral, London, but there is no indication as to whether or not he attended.

Conor did accept the invitation he received from CEMA to show works in their exhibition of Contemporary Ulster Art which opened on 16 June 1951 at the Municipal Museum and Art Gallery, Belfast. His works hung were *The Boy David*, *The Musicians* and *The Two of Us*.

The Scottish Committee of the Arts Council chose for an exhibition of Contemporary Ulster Paintings in Edinburgh in 1951 pictures from the Zoltan Lewinter Frankl collection and four others from the Belfast Municipal Museum and Art Gallery. Four of Conor's pictures from the Frankl collection were shown.

In 1952 William Conor was made an Officer of the Order of the British Empire but, sadly, owing to illness he was unable to attend the Investiture at Buckingham Palace.

He had designed the dust cover for his friend Lynn Doyle's *A Bowl of*

62. The dust jacket for Lynn Doyle's *Ballygullion Bus* published by Gerald Duckworth in 1957.

*Broth* (a rather poor black and white drawing of a young girl spooning broth from a bowl) published by Gerald Duckworth, London, in 1945; now, in October 1956, he accepted Doyle's invitation to design the dust cover for his proposed omnibus volume, *The Ballygullion Bus*. The two following letters from Duckworths show that an artist does not have complete artistic freedom but is limited by the ideas of the publishers and their preference for simpler and cheaper printing techniques.

Our idea was an old Irish country bus with various local characters, (including, if possible, your own admirable version of Mr. Murphy) running to catch it; but, of course, we leave it to you how the people are introduced. We should like a spacious Irish countryside background with a good deal of sky at the top on which we can typeset the title with the Author's name so as to save you the trouble of lettering.

I enclose a wrapper of ours, the orange part of which will be almost the same size as Lynn Doyle's book. We can give you exact dimensions later, but would be glad of some kind of pencil rough in advance for approval. January 31st for the finished job is good enough for us.

If you can work in 3 or 4 flat colours that makes it easier and cheaper for us: but if not, no great matter.

From a letter dated January 1957:

It is excellent and, we think, will do the job exactly as it should be done. I have three comments only:
1. Since your bowler-hatted Patrick Murphy (attached) is now so famous, and he is the key to this book too, could he be the figure with one step on the bus, about to get in?
2. Could the word 'Ballygullion' appear small but just distinguishable on a board on the side of the bus?
3. Isn't the left leg of the girl on the left of the picture a bit out of the drawing?

We should like to use Mr. Murphy (as attached) as a colour frontispiece for the book, since we still have the colour blocks for him, and pay you fifteen guineas instead of the ten first proposed? Do you approve? I feel sure this is what Mr. Montgomery would like.

## Introspection

When John Irvine suggested to his publisher, William Carter of H. R. Carter Publications, that William Conor would be the ideal person to commission to illustrate the dust jacket for his book *By Winding Roads* (published 1950), a successful meeting was arranged at Mooney's, a bar on the Malone Road, Belfast, much frequented by literary people. This was the first occasion on which William Carter and William Conor had met; the meeting was a fortunate one for Conor, who had been going through a difficult period suffering greatly from depression, wondering whether all the work he had done up to that time had been really worth while. It was through the persuasion and encouragement of friends that he started to work again and the completion in 1950 of a commissioned portrait of Lord Farnham for the Grand Masonic Lodge of Ireland, was the first work he had done in a year or more. This was followed by the dust jacket for the John Irvine book which proved to be a major step

Plate 1. *Children of Ulster*. Early 1930s approx. Oil on canvas.
104.2 × 74.9 cms
George and Maura McClelland collection, Dublin.

63. *By Winding Roads.*
1950. Wax crayon on paper.
45.7 × 36.8 cms
Mr William Carter.
(This was used as the dust
jacket illustration for John
Irvine's *By Winding Roads.*)

Plate 2 *Off to the Starting.
Gate.*
N.d. Oil on canvas.
45.1 × 35.6 cms
George and Maura
McClelland collection,
Dublin.

towards recovery, renewing his zest for his work. This is thought to be one of his last totally original drawings as he was now mostly relying on his early sketches.

For William Carter this meeting was the beginning of a close friendship especially as both men lived near to one another in the Antrim Road area of Belfast. It soon became the custom for Conor to visit the Carter family perhaps three or four evenings a week, asking if Carter was going over to the 'Club' (the Ulster Arts Club, then in premises in Great Victoria Street, Belfast, later moving to the Lisburn Road). Conor liked the security of going with William Carter, knowing that he would get home safely without worrying about public transport.

At that time William Carter was travelling to Dublin almost monthly on business, staying two or three days at a time. It became the custom for Conor to accompany him on the journey, staying with friends such as Leslie Montomgery (Lynn Doyle) who lived at Malahide or Robert M. Smyllie, editor of the *Irish Times*, who lived at Delgany. The delivery

64. *Malahide, Co Dublin*.
N.d. Wax crayon on paper.
34.3 × 44.5 cms
George and Maura
McClelland Collection,
Dublin.

point was, however, always in Dublin. William Carter recalls:

> Conor would go to the Pearl Bar, Fleet Street, opposite the side entrance to the *Irish Times*, and Mr. Smyllie would be installed at his table with interesting and well known people. We never approached the table directly, we would get a drink at the bar and wait until we were noticed and then we would be beckoned over and Smyllie, who was terribly fond of William Conor would look at him very sternly and Willie nervously fiddling with his coat button would rarely wait for Smyllie to speak first and Smyllie would scold him about something in an affectionate way. Smyllie would even detail some young fellow from the *Irish Times*, who, when it was time for the last bus to Delgany or the last train to Malahide, according to where Conor was staying, would scour the places where the artist was to be found and put him on the bus or train.
>
> Conor would always like to see Brinsley MacNamara who was Registrar of the National Gallery in Dublin and one of the circle of friends and acquaintances, but he was a person who would take 'a scunner' against a particular meeting place from time to time, as did John Irvine, so one had to find out where he was going.

Brinsley MacNamara, the pen name of John Weldon, published in 1918 his first book *The Valley of the Squinting Windows*, a realistic novel of rural life. He continued to write novels and also plays which were staged at the Abbey Theatre.

Through Robert (Bertie) Smyllie's association with Delgany Golf Club, Conor was made an Honorary Member, although he was not a golfer.

On one occasion William Carter declined to join Conor for a social evening because he wanted an early night; next day, Conor told him with great glee of the marvellous time he'd had, tumbling out names of famous people including a film star and, 'There was you in your hotel reading your Bible!'

William Carter cannot remember anyone disliking Conor:

He was a very lovable person and his simplicity veiled great depth of understanding of human nature and of people, he got to essentials in a very simple way and he had a tremendous tolerance of people except for a bore, practically anything else was excusable. He would talk about a person affectionately as a rascal, but a likable rascal, but a bore was a bore and beyond the Pale. He was a very self-effacing person except when it came to his position as an artist. I think a number of people have observed that when he was talking seriously about art and he wanted to express his own opinion authoritatively he didn't say 'I' he said Conor. He would talk about himself in the third person as though he were two people, he was Willie Conor the person and he was Conor the artist, for whom he had considerable respect. I remember the Ulster Arts Club had an exhibition of members' work, including one Conor oil, which was for sale. Conor usually felt miserable at exhibitions as he hated having to stand about and try to talk with people he didn't like or know, being very bad at it, the complete opposite to a salesman. Someone was very interested in purchasing his painting and said to Willie, 'I like that, it's very good,' to which Willie replied, 'Odd you should say that because William Conor says I should not have allowed it to be put up on the wall at all'.

He held strong views about the reproduction of paintings, views clearly expressed in an article in the *Sunday Press*, 10 February 1968:

Although William Conor made very little money from his work until he was well on in life, he was very firm about one thing. Even when he had become

65. *Dublin Culture*, by Alan Reeve, reproduced from an undated cutting from the *Irish Times*, Dublin among the Conor papers.
The original cartoon still hangs in the Palace Bar, Dublin.

POETS' PUB. Under the title " Dublin Culture," this cartoon, by the New Zealand caricaturist, Alan Reeve, was published in the " Irish Times " in 1940. The setting is the back room of the Palace Bar, Fleet street. The names are as follows:—BACK ROW (from left-hand corner) John P. Colbert (with pipe). G. H. Burrows, Francis MacManus, Maurice Walsh. (Standing) Patrick Kavanagh. (Centre back) Brian O'Nolan. Liam Redmond, Donagh MacDonagh. (Standing) John Chichester. (Seated, right-hand corner) Austin Clarke, Padraic Fallon, F. R. Higgins. MIDDLE ROW (from left): (Standing, with camera) Alec Newman. (Seated, at table below camera) Ewart Milne (from left) R. C. Ferguson, Esmonde Little, R. M. Smyllie, Brinsley MacNamara. (Below) William Conor. (Looking at book) Seamus Lynn Doyle, Leslie Yodaiken, Roibeard O Farachain, M. J. MacManus (in black hat). (Standing) Tom, one of the barmen. Centre table O'Sullivan Right-hand table (at top) Cathal O'Shannon, Jerome Connor, David Sears. (At bottom) George Leitch, Desmond Rushton BOTTOM ROW (from left): Alan Reeve (black suit and beard), G. J. C. Tynan-O'Mahony, A. J. Leventhal, Edward Sheehy. Centre table (front) Patrick O'Connor, Harry Kernoff, Sean O'Sullivan. Bottom (right) Jack, Sean and Mick.

66. *The Hurley Players*.
1948 approx. Crayon on paper.
61 × 50.8 cms
Ulster Folk Museum
Collection.

acknowledged and famous, he would never agree to having even the best reproductions made of his paintings in order to cash in on what would have been a 'lucrative outlet' to meet a growing popular demand.

His objection in principle to this practice was, 'Every painting is a unique creation, even with its own individual errors and flaws'. He felt that mass production under-valued the individuality of the artist's work.

He was firmly of the opinion that it would be far better if people would patronize the arts, not by coveting mere imitations of the best, but by hanging originals of working artists on their walls, even if they did not qualify as masterpieces.

The only concession he made to this principle was to allow the occasional reproduction of his painting in book form.

Even with his strong views about art Conor could be very matter of fact, even careless, with his own sketches. He rarely dated his works, and often left them unsigned. When James Black, Headmaster of Hopefield School, asked Conor to sign one of the drawings he had acquired from him, Conor picked up the nearest crayon and signed his name in a colour which clashed with the rest of the picture; it would have stayed that way if he had not been made to go over the signature with an appropriate coloured crayon. Some years later, when Conor paid a visit to the School to see the art classes and talk with the pupils he was very impressed with the art materials with which they were provided and with the space and light in which they could work as compared with his day.

In 1956 Bray Urban District Council purchased for their Public Library William Conor's *Fluter's Tune*, an oil painting which has always been one of the most popular with the Library readers. At that time the Irish Arts Council was giving grants at the rate of fifty per cent of the purchase price of paintings and pieces of sculpture to Local Authorities who were interested in acquiring the works of Irish artists.

For Conor, the meetings with friends continued over Christmas and he was drawn into warm family gatherings which brought him much pleasure, especially in homes where there were children. On Christmas Eve he would call with William and Joan Carter and was delighted to share in the atmosphere of bustle and preparation and the decoration of the Christmas tree after the children had gone to bed.

On Christmas mornings he would be one of the many who would gather to exchange greetings and enjoy hospitality at the home of the Hayward family who held open house for their friends. On one such occasion William seemed to be enjoying greatly a particular variety of canapé. At last he summoned up the courage to go to his host and enquire what it was. 'That is caviar,' he was told. 'Oh!' said Conor. 'Well, tell me, what exactly is caviar?' This was explained to him and a look of dismay crossed his face. Then, after a pause he said, 'I was enjoying it that much I wish I hadn't asked. That's what you get for asking questions.'

Conor recalled this incident on many occasions and with obvious delight.

# 10

# THE
# HARVEST YEARS

A retrospective Conor exhibition was held by the Council for the Encouragement of Music and the Arts in 1957, at the Museum and Art Gallery, Belfast, and was opened by Lady Wakehurst. Altogether there were one hundred and fifty-one paintings exhibited, covering his output over the previous forty-five years. Seventy-six of the works were owned by the artist; the others were mainly owned by Ulster people, while a few came from the Republic of Ireland, the Manchester City Art Gallery and the Whitworth Art Gallery. Seventy-nine of the pictures were oils, the rest were watercolour and drawing in various media.

In the same year he became President of the Royal Ulster Academy, a position which he held until 1964. Rowel Friers, a close friend as well as Vice-President for a time during Conor's Presidency, told me that although Conor

> was reluctant to be President . . . he really was a good President because he was the most distinguished artist we had, but as far as being a President he wasn't really interested . . . I mean he called it a lot of tomfoolery. He preferred just to get on with his work or sit with his pals and talk . . . but he wasn't the sort of man who would be standing up there proudly with his chain of office on him making big speeches. He could hardly get a speech out when he stood on his feet. . . . His speeches were all merely sitting round a table and chatting but they were good years while he was President and the Academy took a lot of big steps forward then and has improved tremendously since that day.

The Royal Ulster Academy Exhibition of 1958, which was opened by His Excellency The Lord Wakehurst, Governor of Northern Ireland, was the first to benefit from the changes that had been instigated in the

67. Conor at home working on his oil painting of *The Gypsy Girl*.
Photograph taken by Mr Reggie McClure in 1964.

previous months. A committee of seven appointed by the Academy had reduced sharply the number of works chosen for exhibition and the usual three spacious galleries for two hundred works became three walls for the display of forty exhibits.

Conor's Presidential speech drew attention to these changes:

Of recent years maledictions have been heaped on the head of the R.U.A. Nevertheless, it is not hostile to criticism, in fact, it takes regard to what is said and knows that true and sincere work of art greeted with enthusiastic abuse may be a tribute; abuse like hearty applause may be excited by work that has behind it sound conviction. Anyhow, the Academy itself felt it was tending toward a little smugness and self-complacency and unless something was done it would be sucked into a backwater, become impotent, insignificant and provincial. So a selection committee was appointed with full powers to make drastic reductions on work submitted for exhibition. These changes are regrettable, but as you know perfection is not of this world, and general merit can only be achieved by great sacrifices.

In this topsy turvy age, when everyone is shouting 'forward', and no one is expected to ask 'where' it would seem as if nothing matters or rather, it matters nothing what the artist paints or sculpts, and the artists themselves are so fiercely individualistic that they don't know what each other is getting at. Sometimes I think the artist, as an honest and skilled craftsman, is quickly disappearing and it would seem that the very deficiencies in work today are seized upon as something very novel and original.

Art exists only where things are made to last forever.

Every now and then he would pack a few things and head for London: 'It is refreshing to get away, just to see what's going on in the artistic world. We are just a little backward here'. It was on one of these trips to London, while he was still President of the Royal Ulster Academy, that he visited a Picasso exhibition at the Tate Gallery. He came away from it with with 'an open mind'. The exhibition was crowded when he went through and he confesses that he found as much interest in the people as in the pictures. 'They were mostly young with an average age of about twenty-five and their response seemed to be curiously unemotional – they looked at the pictures and did not know what to say and I, too, did not know in many cases.'

It was in 1957 that the Queen's University of Belfast conferred on Conor the Honorary Degree of Master of Arts, as a token of appreciation for his distinction as an artist in Northern Ireland. His pleasure in this is recorded in his self-portrait 'gowned' as Master of Arts.

68. Conor and his sister Mary walking in Dublin.
Photograph from the Conor papers.

From the early fifties the years began to take their toll of the family: Martin died on 3 August 1952, and John on the 13 March 1953; both were bachelors and died at home. Nor was Mary very well. Now she was beginning to find the burdens of family and domestic responsibilities heavier than before. It must have been of natural concern to a sister so loving and reliable that she was unable to cope with the strains. William and Russell were greatly worried about her and eventually it became necessary for her to enter a private nursing home nearby where she died, not long afterwards, from cerebral thrombosis on 18 April 1958, at the age of eighty.

Now more than ever before the two brothers appreciated the continuing kindness of friends, especially being able to spend each Christmas Day with the Carter family, with whom they felt so much at home.

An opportunity arose in May 1959 for Conor to sell his work to an American couple, Mr and Mrs Hugh Hyde, who were friends of Lord Wakehurst, the Patron of CEMA. They were interested in collecting works by artists from the North of Ireland for sale to the American public from their Spook Farm Gallery, New Jersey. But correspondence with Mrs Hyde reveals that slides sent to them did not include any works by William Conor. In any case, this project fell through as shipping charges were too great and the Hydes were at that time unable to come over and view the works.

In the same year Conor was granted on behalf of the Government of Northern Ireland a Civil List pension by the Minister of Finance, Captain Terence O'Neill, in recognition of his 'meritorious public service to the cause of fine arts in Northern Ireland'. From the Society of Ulster Architects came commendations from Architect Members for the inclusion of two non-subscribing members, Lord Antrim and William Conor, to serve on the jury to select the winner of the Royal Institute of British Architects' Bronze Medal.

His studio at 11a Stranmillis Road, Belfast, which he had occupied since 1944, had gradually become too great a responsibility for him. He was finding it difficult to make decisions and was probably very relieved when, in 1959, friends persuaded him to give it up and move his paintings and drawings to his home at 107 Salisbury Avenue and to work from there.

Rowel Friers has told me that this large room with a sloping glass roof could have been an excellent studio, but it was impossible to maintain a working heat during the winter. When it rained, the tins and buckets placed about the room catching drops of water coming in from the roof created a musical accompaniment for this small-figured artist who added to the humorous situation by wearing 'a long blue smock which resembled a blue tent'.

Surrounding him would be masses of his work, drawings and canvasses which he would sometimes ask his friends to sort through and select those they thought he should try and sell. John Hewitt has told me that 'at times this could be difficult as he was sensitive to criticism even though it might only be preferring one work to another'.

Ulster Television, pursuing its policy of supporting local artists,

writers, actors and musicians, not only through publicity but also by material help, had some dealings with William Conor in 1961, when he had called with R. B. Henderson, Managing Director of Ulster Television, and offered him two pictures, one a forceful crayon drawing *At the Races* and the other a less immediately recognisable example of his work in watercolour and crayon, a scenic picture entitled *Still Waters*, which Conor said was of the Minnowburn near Shaw's Bridge, Belfast. The sum of £20 which Conor had asked was increased by the Board to 46 guineas for the purchase of these pictures. R. B. Henderson recalled that this was a rare and pleasurable business negotiation, as he and William Conor had been friends for years and had had the pleasure of an evening together in 1950, in Dublin, 'under the benign and huge presence of Mr Smyllie who was then Editor of the *Irish Times*.'

An exhibition of paintings by William Conor and other Ulster artists, which was presented by CEMA in association with Dungannon Urban and Rural District Councils, was held in the library of the Royal School, Dungannon in February 1962. Of those exhibited, thirteen were by Conor, among them *The Body Blow*, *Rowing to the Mainland* and *Armagh Cathedral*.

On the 25 May 1963, the Ulster Arts Club exhibition opened at the Ulster Museum, Belfast. Conor exhibited five works: *The Darling*, *Oh What Can the Matter Be?*, *Nine Busy Fingers*, *Mill Girls* and *An Only Child*.

The Royal Ulster Academy on 8 May 1964 gave a dinner in honour of William Conor on the occasion of his eighty-third birthday and forthcoming retirement as their President. It was a most successful evening; the menu card was illustrated with five of Conor's small lino cuts, one being *The Peace Maker*. After Patric Stevenson, another local artist and the then Secretary of the Academy, proposed the Toast to Conor, he presented him with three gifts, one of them a tribute in verse written by him and illustrated on vellum by Mercy Hunter.

In October of that year Richard Hayward died in a motor accident. Mrs Fowweather recalls, when she saw Conor the following week, how much this death had upset him. He felt that somehow it marked the beginning of the end, that the shadows were lengthening and darkening, and he remarked to her, 'It makes you wonder what it's all about'. It was while speaking with Mrs Fowweather and her mother (the late Florence McDowell) on this occasion – and perhaps more than usually conscious of the loss of friends and the suddenness of change – that he took from his sketch book a drawing of his companions during the early years at Bridge House and, handing it to her, said, 'Here, you better have this'.

Before the end of that year Conor lent Ulster Television Limited a portfolio of his work to illustrate the beginning and end of each programme in the series 'The Humour is on me Now'. These sketches were greatly appreciated by many people 'as they were just right for establishing the mood'.

Often he would remark on his dislike for public speaking, feeling he had not the same mastery over words as with his art. He said of words: 'I feel about them what the old farmer said about his donkey – "It's a

69. Conor in his studio 1958. Photograph from the Conor papers.

dacent baste,'' said he, ''an' it's a willin' baste – but it's thrawn''.' In preparing a speech Conor would either write it out completely in block capitals or else write the first few words of each of the points he wanted to make. From the written notes he has left about art in general or his own work, we can see how full of refreshing commonsense he was.

The following small incident reflects Conor's gentle sense of humour. On one occasion when called upon to speak at an exhibition, he got up and while standing searching through his pockets he said, 'I don't quite know what I'm going to say to you ladies and gentlemen. I was thinking of some ideas on the way over and jotted down one or two notes on my bus ticket and now I'm sorry to say I seem to have lost it, so I'll just have to say a few words without notes.'

An exhibition of forty-one of William Conor's works opened on the 7 December 1964, at the Bell Gallery in Alfred Street, Belfast. Of these, twenty-two were drawings and the rest oils, including *Gather Round Friends*, *Myself When Young* and *The Only Child*.

In 1965, Nelson Bell, of the Bell Gallery, organised a representative exhibition of Ulster art, staged in Selfridges Gallery, London, to run for one week from 1 March, in connection with an 'Ulster Fortnight', which the store gave to boost Ulster products. The artists included were: William Conor, Maurice Wilks, R. Taylor Carson, Patric Stevenson, Olive Henry, Max MacCabe, Kathleen Bell, Frank McKelvey, Kenneth Webb, Rowland Hill, Malcolm Bennett, Ian Pakenham, Renee Bickerstaff, Donald McPherson and Lawrence MacKenna. It was not a success in the terms of picture sales; one of the reasons may have been that the prices suggested by the artists were increased by Selfridges. The only work sold was a picture by Kenneth Webb.

Victoria College, Belfast, held a small exhibition of his work in this same year in the 'Studio', the art room of the old school buildings in Lower Crescent and I am sorry that I was not then one of the pupils to whom he explained some of his feelings about Modern Art. And it is to the then art mistress Miss Mercy Hunter that I owe this transcription of a tape which she recorded on that occasion.

I am not a modern painter so, therefore, I feel that it is not my duty to explain it. I was never brought up to work in the manner of modern art. I was taught more [*sic*] less representative I don't think it would be wise of me to explain, you see I remember well I was at an exhibition where some women were passing round and I remember standing at a picture which I liked very much, it was of a child's head and I thought it was beautifully painted, a bit photographic but nevertheless a work of art. I remember a woman who seemed to be leading the group, they were all admiring this painting and she said, 'Yes, it's quite good' but dismissed it, 'Oh! it's Victorian', but that's wrong, it's only a label. 'Is it a work of art?' was the question; to me it doesn't matter what label she put on it, and I should have liked to have asked her that but that was only a test. It doesn't matter otherwise but that's the trouble, we are all becoming label fixers now anyhow. Edwardian or Victorian or something else, you see there have never been so many Schools of Painting, I have noticed in my own time, they all flourished for a time and then vanished, dozens of them . . .

92

A Memorial Fund Exhibition consisting of works donated by artists was held in May 1965 at the Bell Gallery for the benefit of the family of the late Sam Thompson, the shipyard worker who wrote *Over the Bridge* and *The Evangelist*. Catalogue No. 13 was Conor's *Polling Day*.

The Exhibition of Great Irishmen held in the Ulster Museum for one month from 24 June 1965 included two oil portraits by Conor: *Charles Stewart Henry Vane-Tempest-Stewart, 7th Marquis of Londonderry 1878-1949*, lent by The Queen's University of Belfast, and the *Reverend James Brown Armour 1841–1928*, lent by Magee University College, Londonderry.

An exhibition of his work was also opened on 9 December 1965, at the Botanic Inn, Belfast, in which his oil painting *Songs of Praise* was one of the works hung.

Two months later, in February 1966, the Bell Gallery held an exhibition of Conor's work entitled 'Belfast of Yesterday'. Kenneth Jamison, who wrote the foreword to the catalogue, mentions one of my favourite stories of how, 'unable to pay the admission, he [Conor]

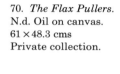

70. *The Flax Pullers*.
N.d. Oil on canvas.
61 × 48.3 cms
Private collection.

71. *The Old Woman.*
N.d. Oil on canvas.
29.2 × 22.9 cms
Private collection.

insinuated himself into the Maze races, through a barbed wire fence, tearing the back-side out of his trousers on the way, and was featured next day in the Social and Personal as one of the distinguished people at the meeting'. There were 77 pictures in all: 55 drawings, 13 watercolours and 9 oils. It was a tremendous success; by the end of the first week 67 of the pictures had been sold – even so Conor remained modest and said of the exhibition that,'It reflects my interpretation of the life of industry and people of Belfast forty or fifty years ago. It was an interesting period and I think that has a good deal to do with it, I believe it is one of my most successful'.

Among those who met him from time to time at exhibitions, one or two have recalled that his brown eyes reflected the warmth and humour of the man and that, in conversation, his glance would dart round the company so that everyone in the circle would feel included in what he was saying, and that when he chuckled the laughter was in his eyes too. During this exhibition Conor, moving among the many who were there, remarked that a number of the pictures exhibited he had 'for one reason or another not parted with until now' and that recently he had been 'going through them and had spent some time working on them and touching them up'.

It was while the Lord Mayor of Belfast, Councillor Sir William Jenkins, JP, was opening this exhibition on 24 February, that he invited Conor to have his eighty-fifth birthday celebrations at the City Hall, bringing with him as many of his friends as he liked. The celebrations took place on 7 May, which Conor thought was his birth date; in fact, his real birthday was two days later. Mercy Hunter, whom Conor invited as his lady guest, remembers it as being 'a most enjoyable luncheon'.

In the Spring of 1966 an interesting exhibition of selected pictures and sculptures from the W. A. N. MacGeough Bond collection was on view at the Ulster Museum, Belfast. It included two pictures by William

94

Conor, *The Fiddler* (No. 12) an oil on canvas stuck on board (earlier exhibited in 1936 (No. 277) at the Royal Institute of Oil Painters) and *Donegal Dancer* (No. 13), a chalk drawing on paper which was originally in the Lynn Doyle Collection.

The following year, on 9 November, the Bell Gallery held a ten day exhibition entitled 'Conor', presenting thirty-eight of his works, sixteen oils and twenty-two drawings, covering at least fifty years of his painting career. Of those exhibited were the oil portrait of *The Warden, Picture House Queue, The Stitching Factory, Courtin', Bugler of the Old Castle Guards, Children Skipping, Belfast 1912, Fruit Sellers* and *The Boxing Bout.* The exhibition was opened by the Countess of Antrim.

It gave Conor much pleasure to take part in 'Today and Yesterday in Northern Ireland: People at Work', a series of BBC radio broadcasts for schools. The programme transmitted on 22 March 1968 and produced by Douglas Carson, included Sam Hanna Bell as interviewer and narrator and Kenneth Jamison as critic. The pamphlet for the

Spring Term broadcasts also contained twelve illustrations of Conor's work.

In the family life of this compassionate man, who had remained a bachelor, there would seem to be little doubt of how deeply felt had been the emotional loss he had suffered in the death of his mother in 1933. His devotion to her had been such that the comment 'almost Marian', made by William Carter, seems but to emphasize the full acceptance of the 'maternal' in his life, and this is reflected, not only in his masterpiece of portraiture, that of his mother in old age, but in almost all of his pictures depicting mother and child and in the quality of tenderness that is inherent in his portrayals of children.

After this time there were the years of achievement and ever increasing recognition. Always in the background, keeping alive the warmth and emotional security of the home, was his sister Mary, also loved, respected and trusted as his mother had been. With her death in 1958 William Conor suffered another deep bereavement which left him, at the age of seventy-seven, very lonely and, with his last remaining brother, Russell, declining slowly into senility. The home in which the two brothers for so long had had Mary's care and comfort gradually became over the next ten years little more than a cold and untended house.

The dismal conditions of their existence towards the end of their lives are vividly described by Rowel Friers:

It was rather sad to see them, the two old men in this big, big house – which was far to big for them – sitting with their overcoats on, huddled round a fire – an electric fire with one bar going and it sparking at the side about to go out altogether – in fact, very dangerous. Many a time I went in and found that they had no food, and went out and got them some – made them a fry or went out and got chips and fish for them, or whatever – and they would be delighted with that. In fact, I don't know how they existed at all, together, in this way, with no one to look after them. They did have a help who came in to clean up, but that was about all they did. In fact, very often when you looked at the house you wouldn't have thought they'd done that either – Billy had quite a wee bit of money himself – I mean, one would have thought he had no money, but he ended up with a few thousand . . . So it was rather sad to think that they had this amount of money and they never really used it, and they could have lived so much more comfortably with someone looking after them.

Further comment comes from James Vitty:

During his later years I visited Willie often at his home in Salisbury Avenue, which was managed by his sister, Mary, and his brother Russell lived there as well. There was a very close relationship between the three of them but Mary was the boss and ran a lovely house. After Mary died I'm afraid the conditions of this house deteriorated at a terrible rate. It got so bad in the end that some of us decided that one of us would have to go up one night each week, on a form of rota, and see that both Russell and Willie had a meal and were put in bed properly. We also ordered central heating to be installed in the house and engaged a housekeeper to start the following week. Unfortunately, Willie died before any of these things could be put into operation.

With his brother's further decline in health and eventual removal to a nursing home, William Conor had to accept alone the day-to-day

Plate 3. *The Artists' Mother*. N.d. Watercolour on paper. 43.2 × 34.3 cms Private collection.

73. *Trees on the Lagan.*
1935 approx. Oil on canvas.
50.8 × 40.6 cms
Ulster Folk Museum
Collection.

Plate 4. *The Blind Fiddler.*
1937 approx. Oil on canvas.
50.8 × 40.6 cms
George and Maura
McClelland collection,
Dublin.

responsibilities and cares of living, though he continued to have the affectionate concern and help of his friends, whom he met as usual for coffee and talk at the Chalet D'Or or in the nearby Linen Hall Library.

Earlier one of the most popular meeting places for those interested in the arts – painters, writers, actors from the nearby Group Theatre and from the BBC – was a restaurant in the centre of Belfast, situated directly opposite to the City Hall where the Halifax Building Society office now stands. Mrs Zoltan Lewinter-Frankl sometimes went there with her husband, the art collector and connoisseur, and she remembers it as 'a Coffee House in those days called Campbell's . . . and every Saturday morning everybody of artistic name was meeting here – it was a lovely morning . . . everybody telling what they had done during the week . . . mostly painters and writers . . . Jack Loudan, W. R. Rodgers, are names I remember . . . Denis Ireland and Nevin Foster . . .'

There were those who might have had a memory of perhaps only an occasional meeting which, however, remained bright in the mind. One such was Richard MacCullagh, who speaks of 'having had coffee with William Conor in Campbell's cafe . . . Across the way the flower girls sold their wares . . . Belfast for Conor was no mean city . . . Time submerges the past but Conor had stayed the hand of Time and saved an epoch for us before it was lost . . . this was 1960.'

The meeting place eventually changed to the Chalet D'Or, also known as the Stepaside, and for several of the crowd the meetings were daily – Willie Conor, Jimmy Vitty, Jim Gracey, Padraic Woods, Jim Ryan, Herbert Bell, Ren Sharp, J. J. Campbell, Patrick Riddell, Maurice Shanks, Ralph 'Bud' Bossence, Joe Tomelty, John Boyd, Sam Hanna Bell and often Rowel Friers.

Jack Loudan was later to recall in the *Belfast Telegraph* an incident which happened to Conor of how

> one morning a waitress, scarcely more than a child, spilt some coffee on his trousers. When she watched him telling me about this a few minutes later she came to the table and said, 'Do you know what you are? You're an oul' clashbeg.' Nothing could have pleased him more. It was friendly acceptance by one of his own Ulster people, more important than praise from a higher level. It was as if one of his own creations had spoken to him from the canvas.

The giving up of his studio at Stranmillis in 1959 had meant a partial change in the pattern of his day; now, his work was done at home, in his own time, copying or retouching old canvases. These quieter hours may have deepened the thoughts and questionings which over the years he had continued to voice to one or two close personal friends about the meaning of life, the value of his work, an ultimate confirmation . . .

During an evening spent with Herbert Bell and only two days before his sudden death Conor spoke briefly of these feelings. The broken sentences – disconnected – read like thoughts spoken aloud to himself.

> CONOR: I wasn't any use to anybody . . .
> H.B.: You will be to the people of Northern Ireland . . .
> CONOR: But what do they care? . . .
> I knew well, many, many years ago, that when I showed in London and elsewhere the people of Belfast were thinking I was showing them as poor, humble people, wearing shawls and dungarees . . . I know that . . .
> Is there a purpose or meaning in 'Life'? . . . Why have I been living so long? Is there any meaning in that? I lived a life similar to many. I drank a lot . . . Women . . . No . . . Not much of that.
> I was born and bred a Presbyterian but it means nothing.

Here again William Carter has made a thoughtful contribution.

> William was seldom assertive and when he did dogmatize it was generally on some aspect of art about which he felt deeply. On such occasions he would speak in the third person, saying 'Conor thinks . . .'
> I believe this separation in his mind of Conor the respected artist from the shy man who worried about inadequacy in handling the minor problems of living is important. It was something he shared with many friends of his own generation. Lynn Doyle could be less conventional in his behaviour than bank manager Leslie Montgomery. Richard Rowley could in verse question the social and economic system supported by the handkerchief manufacturer and Union Club member R. V. Williams. Seamus O'Sullivan dominating his circle in the Palace Bar was a different man from the Wesleyan Methodist pharmaceutical chemist James Sullivan Starkey. William went only a tiny step towards adopting a pseudonym, dropping the second 'n' from his surname but even this was enough to create dichotomy.
> Arising from this, there was William Connor the Presbyterian and his alter ego William Conor the agnostic. William's frequent declarations of his

74. *The Farmers' Race.*
1932 approx. Crayon on paper.
61 × 50.8 cms
Ulster Folk Museum
Collection.

Presbyterianism were to identify the tradition into which he had been born and because he was sensitive that his 'papish' appearance and name led those who did not know him to think he dug with the wrong foot. The Presbyterian Church had not, I think, any religious message for him. But in the closing years of his life he desperately wanted assurance that Conor with the one 'n' was immortal. He would have been an easy target for a charismatic proselytiser were it not that the other Connor would have shrunk in horror from the stigma of having 'turned'.

It was with a sense of shock and sincere grief that his friends and the general public heard of his death on 6 February 1968, at the age of 87 at his home in Salisbury Avenue. Russell, the last surviving member of the family about whom William had been so concerned, had been taken to a nursing home only a week before the artist's death and died there six weeks later on 17 March.

James Vitty explained to me the circumstances of his death, probably from hypothermia. The evening of 5 February was bitterly cold and as Conor went out to the coal-house in the back yard to fill the coal scuttle, he collapsed and died at the back door. Although he was not found until the following morning, it was the opinion that he had died during the evening. It is ironical that arrangements were already under way for central heating to be installed in the house.

Among those who paid tribute to William Conor at the funeral service at Townsend Street Presbyterian Church, Belfast, were the Prime

Minister, Captain Terence O'Neill, who read the lesson, the Minister of Development, Mr Fitzsimmons, many of his artist friends and, representing the theatre, J. G. Devlin, Joe Tomelty and John McBride. The President of the Arts Council of Northern Ireland, Captain Peter Montgomery, flew back from London to attend the service. Wallace Adair Connor and his sister, Mrs Edith Sykes, Conor's nephew and niece, came over from England to join other members of the family. The Minister of Townsend Street Church, the Reverend Rupert Gibson, said in his sermon that if Conor 'had lived on the Continent or perhaps in another age, he would have achieved even more universal fame, but he preferred to live in this Province. Because of this Ulster is richer'.

He was an artist who produced an abundance of work which showed how much he loved not only Belfast and its people but the whole Province; even in death he did not forget them. To these people and their future generations he willed his own personal collection, as well as all his sketches and notes.

Under the terms of his will he left the collection to the Belfast Society for the Promotion of Knowledge (the Linen Hall Library). James Vitty, who was then the Librarian of the Library, and is an Executor of William Conor's estate, commented in the *Sunday News*, 29 December 1968:

> This gesture is typical of William. The pictures include some of his best work, the ones he could not bear to part with during his lifetime. But he loved this country and he felt that this was his best way of showing it.

Not only did he leave works on canvas, but in paper carrier bags; there were at least 800 sketches, on loose pages of his sketch books, the backs of Red Cross war posters, scraps of paper, bill heads, old envelopes and menu cards. Sadly, many were too fragile to mount and frame.

Recognition came late in his life and so it was not until then that he was able to make a reasonable living from his work. In an article by Eddie McIlwaine, 'The Strain at the Top', in *Ireland's Saturday Night* on 11 August 1962, Conor gave his views about the more difficult periods of his life and his reactions to them.

> They never worried me, you see there is no justification for life without art. Since I was a child I knew I just had to paint. There's no other way I could have lived. When you feel like that you are prepared to take the rough with the smooth.
>
> In my young days artists got little encouragement. That has all changed now. People have realised that painting has its part to play.
>
> I suppose my name on a painting means more to-day than it did years ago, but the responsibility doesn't weigh me down too much.
>
> I still enjoy painting. I work at it every day. Then in the evening I sit back with a good book. That's how I relax. I think that's the secret.
>
> When I was younger it might have been different perhaps.
>
> But life isn't as interesting as it used to be. Everything is becoming ready made, and therefore a bit cheap and common.
>
> The trouble is that uniformity is making life too dull.
>
> It is my belief that beauty is never completely absent from the activities of human life.
>
> I have found my best subjects as I wandered around the street. When I see

75. *The Smoothers*.
N.d. Chalk pastel on paper.
47.6 × 30.5 cms
Private collection.

something interesting I stop to draw it on the spot. I work on it later in the studio.

I suppose to some Belfast is ugly and sordid. I never found it so. I never run short of subjects with which to illustrate its industry and the beauty it has for me.

In the Belfast people he tried to 'get the flash of humour which lightens their every day toil, the visual spark which one's wit makes play . . .'

At the 139th Royal Hibernian Academy of Arts at the National College of Art, Kildare Street, Dublin, opened on 6 May 1968, a tribute was paid to William Conor by the inclusion of a small Memorial Exhibition which consisted of six drawings and one oil, *A Sup of Tea*. The Academy relied mainly on works on loan from the Municipal Gallery of Modern Art, Dublin, and from Mrs Kathleen Smyllie, who each lent three works, and one from the artist George Campbell, RHA.

The Royal Ulster Academy included at their Annual Exhibition of

76. *Snow on the Lagan.*
N.d. Oil on hardboard.
34.3 × 43.2 cms sight
Private collection.

that year a memorial show of seven Conor pictures which were lent for the occasion by Mrs Mercy MacCann (Hunter), Mr Harry Cooke Knox, Miss M. Y. Lawrence, and one from the RUA of his Diploma Work. They also introduced a Conor Prize to perpetuate his memory and offered for the first time a yearly monetary award (coupled with a certificate which included an illustration of one of his lino cuts) for an outstanding pictorial work, in any medium, in which a figure(s) is/are the main interest, and which is selected for exhibition. The first winner was F. Cecil Maguire.

Two exhibitions entitled 'William Conor 1881–1968' took place, one on 29 October by the Arts Council of Northern Ireland which consisted of sixty-four works mainly from the Ulster Folk and Transport Museum, the Ulster Museum, the Linen Hall Library and the Arts Council. The other, at William Rodman's in Arthur Street, Belfast, and including L. A. Kaitcer (Antiques), opened on 26 April 1969. Forty-seven works of different media were presented.

A month later the McClelland Galleries, then situated at May Street, Belfast, also held a large exhibition of Conor's pictures. The exhibition of eighty-one works entitled 'Children of Ulster' had originally been organised with Conor's help but was postponed due to his death and was not mounted until after the Arts Council retrospective touring exhibition. McClelland Galleries held in May 1971 an exhibition of Conor's war drawings, 'The Belfast Blitz'; ten of the twenty-seven works were on loan from the Linen Hall Library.

Richard MacCullagh, who sometimes shared a bus seat with William Conor 'as we went up Stranmillis direction where his studio and my College were located', recalls: 'on such occasions my friend would speak "off the cuff". For instance he expressed distaste for the new "glass-box", as he called it, that was built beside the Cathedral as the new College of Art'. Perhaps Conor's opinion might have been redeemed somewhat could he have known that two years after his death the Hall of the College was officially opened by Sir Paul Reilly, Director of the Council of Industrial Design, in January 1970 and named 'The Conor Hall'. James Warwick, the Principal, kindly presented to the College a crayon head and shoulders self-portrait which Conor had given him.

Padraic Woods, whose landscapes also record the past, was a friend who knew William Conor well. He spoke to me of his modesty, his humour and of mutual acquaintances, adding a little personal remembrance – that, when painting or drawing in cold weather, Conor wore comfortable, old-fashioned mittens, which helped to keep his hands warm, while leaving his fingers free to handle brushes or crayons. This was a memory which Mrs Fowweather also recalled, adding that in the later years Conor suffered from arthritis of the hands which often affected his ability to use brushes or crayons with ease, as he was compelled to hold them between his first two fingers.

I also include the tribute (published in the *Irish Weekly*, Belfast, 17 February 1968) which Padraic Woods paid to him:

> William Conor's very agreeable and placid manner, for which he was beloved by everyone, showed you only one side of his character. The other side was a strength and determination of will to work to perfect the great talent that was his. Witness to this dedication is the amount of work to be found to-day in the many galleries, private collections and homes throughout the country. I met Conor many years ago when I was still a student at the College of Art. Since that time we have been very close friends and I have benefited by his advice and help on many occasions.
>
> For many years past a number of friends would meet in the morning over coffee and the seat at the top of the table would be reserved for 'Billy' who would sit there beaming and handing out anecdotes. But he was not always beaming. He would become reflective at times and talk of his friends who had passed away, among them being John Irvine, the Belfast poet, Lynn Doyle, Nevin Foster (Rathcol), Richard Rowley, George MacCann and many others.
>
> He often remarked that he enjoyed the company of literary friends. He didn't like to talk shop. He loved city life but not the lights and rarely explored the country. He painted very few landscapes. The world he loved to portray had all passed away before his own passing. He was a very familiar figure in the city and especially in Fountain Street where the party met and in Wellington Place where he was always given a jocular send-off in the bus by his good friend, Joe Tomelty. We left him to that bus for the last time on Monday at noon when he was in his usual cheerful form and so were we.

The late Dr James Ryan commented in the same article that Conor

77. Joe Tomelty with Conor
boarding the bus.
Photograph from the Conor
papers, taken sometime
between 1965 and 1967.

'often confessed that occasionally he could not afford to buy the
materials necessary for his work as an artist, but he never complained'.

I have found to an increasing extent that the painter and his works
are bonded as one. This is illustrated in an extract from a letter written
by Conor in 1923 to the Manchester City Art Gallery.

Your letter gave me the greatest pleasure, and I consider it a great honour to
have three of my drawings hung in your magnificent permanent collection.
    My friend Williams has already told me of his interview with you, and of the
very flattering things you have been kind enough to say about my work
perhaps it is not too much to say, that your personal interest is even more
valuable to me, than your purchase of my drawings.

A fine tribute was paid by Leslie Montgomery (Lynn C. Doyle), in his book *The Spirit of Ireland*, pp. 104–105.

William Conor has, with his art, done more for his native City of Belfast, than has been done for any other city in the United Kingdom; giving permanence in works of masterly draughtsmanship and colouring to Belfast's humbler streets and to a whole generation of the workers, by whose hands the glory of Belfast has been exalted.

Now his pictures can be viewed as through a window on a part of our past and a preservation of something of our local identity. For this surely we must be grateful. I am.

It is fitting that this part of the book should close with these words written by William Conor:

All my life I have been completely absorbed and with affection in the activities of the Belfast people and surrounding country. Being a Belfast man myself it has been my ambition to reveal the Spiritual Character of its people in all vigour, in all its senses of life, in all its variety, in all its passion, humanity and humour. Since childhood I have wandered its streets, seeing what human value there was to be found around me. These paintings and drawings are not a succession of novelties, nor tiresomely abstract – they are simply the impressions of the personality of the artist towards his subject, seen and felt on his own and an attempt to reveal the spiritual in these days of no faith or belief in anything, and when we have trampled on the best of the past and sacrificed everything of value to the much vaunted name of progress I trust these paintings and drawings will recall a world that is quickly disappearing and could soon be forgotten.

# CONOR'S
# ART

*by*
*John Hewitt*

When I turn to consider William Conor's work I must begin by declaring my interest, for he was the first man I ever recognised as being a genuine artist. This circumstance is clearly important to one who spent over forty years professionally engaged with art galleries on both sides of the Irish Sea. I have seen innumerable exhibitions and visited many studios in these islands and abroad, yet, of all the artists I have met, Conor remains the archetype, imprinting some sort of ideal or image on my memory and deep in my unconscious.

During my childhood he lived within a quarter of a mile of my home. His black soft hat, his loose tie, his low-slung, broad shoulders, his steady, if rather rolling, unhurried stride made him distinctly individual among the passing people in the street.

Fascinated by this romantic, somewhat mysterious phenomenon, I remember that once as a very small inquisitive boy, I followed him at a discreet distance to find out exactly where he was going when he passed our gate in the direction opposite to Landscape Terrace. In the event my quest ended in something of an anti-climax. Along Cliftonpark Avenue and down the Cliftonville Road he strode; then across the tramlines on the Antrim Road, where, unaccompanied, I was forbidden to venture. Up the steps, then, he headed, through the glass doors of the Lyceum Cinema.

My father often took me to see what was on view on the top floor of the Public Library in Royal Avenue, where the Art Gallery then was. There I saw among the many pictures highly distinctive paintings and drawings by this man who spelled his name with one 'n'; those that I recall most vividly, crayon or chalk drawings of groups of shawl-

78. *Thursday's Child.*
N.d. Oil on canvas.
73.7×61 cms
George and Maura
McClelland Collection,
Dublin.

107

wrapped mill girls such as you could see walking together or stopping to chat on the Shankill or Crumlin Roads.

Later I was taken to the opening of the annual exhibitions of the Belfast Art Society, and I learned to identify and was once or twice introduced to some of the exhibitors. So that when, by the winter of 1930, I went to work in the Art Gallery now at Stranmillis, during the gathering in, the hanging of exhibits and the official openings I came to know then who were considered the leading artists of the community.

It was in those years that I realised more clearly how representative Conor was. Joe Carey, that diffident elderly man in leggings or knickerbockers, painted purple heathery watercolours. His wife was socially the dominant partner. The tweedy Humbert Craig painted billowy clouds and sunlit bogs in the Glens of Antrim where he usually lived. Sharp-featured Frank McKelvey painted wading children at the seashore. Burly neat-bearded Hans Iten painted bluebells at Belvoir or leafy trees along the Lagan towpath – he was a foreigner who, by some necessity of the linen trade, lived here. You could see flower paintings of his in your doctor's waiting room. Miss Praeger, a formidable and dignified lady, lived in Holywood and modelled coy children in clay. That diminutive rowdy John Langtry Lynas was forever creating a scene and stumping out in a temper, his few pictures in conté crayon, the aborted sprouts of his vast imaginings. Little long-nosed Sir John Lavery, formally dressed, was a rare visitant. He painted fashionable or famous people over in London. Conor now lived in Salisbury Avenue and painted and drew the working people of the town. He belonged to us in a very special sense.

## 2

Now when, in May 1981, we celebrate William Conor's centenary, he will have been dead for more than a dozen years, the man himself remembered only by an ever dwindling company. Most of those who have heard his name can only seek out the many works which remain in private hands or in the museums.

As far back as 1922 the art critic of the *Westminster Gazette* nominated him as 'the delineator of Ulster industrialism'. But this tag is too summary. We will need to discover that he was a prolific artist who handled oil and watercolour, greasy crayons, chalks and pencil, producing, besides his working class subjects, portraits officially commissioned or privately ordered, some landscapes, some decorative costume designs, a few flowerpieces, a print or two.

The reader of this volume will have been acquainted with a full account of his life and his career, of items he exhibited, where and when, and to what professional bodies he belonged, and where examples of his work may most readily be found, for Judith Wilson, in her research and in this resultant narrative, has missed nothing of significance.

So, knowing the course of his training and the nature of his work, one might expect to be able to distinguish successive periods in his development. But such an analysis does not spring easily to eye or mind.

To seek the aid of simple chronology is no help in this, for he seldom dated more than a few drawings, frequently changed the titles of paintings from exhibition to exhibition, made late paintings from early sketches, and though his signature may alter over the years, this may not consistently relate to the time that the painting was executed. Another confusion is that at various times he made modified versions of already completed works.

From the evidence of paintings which I had seen in exhibitions I once made the ready assumption that sometime in the early Thirties, weary of his urban themes, he had turned to subjects with a rural setting, field work, village life, the country *ceili*, the country race-meeting, the hurling match. This idea fell into place very neatly with another hypothesis which I had, for which there seemed to be considerable evidence, that, in the Twenties and just before, Belfast and the life in its back streets, its mills, factories, shipyards, had achieved some importance as a source of and subject for creative expression.

Richard Rowley (1877–1947), locally the leading poet of the day, had in his first book, *The City of Refuge* (1917), a long poem entitled 'The City Beautiful' with such lines as 'Stern City! thou grey Mother of mine ... Thy tall mill chimneys' strict columnar line ... Thy great Gantry's gaunt design. . . .' And in a review the *Times Literary Supplement* announced 'The sound of a great Northern manufacturing city vibrates through these poems'.

His second book, explicitly entitled *City Songs* (1918), was even more emphatic in asserting its interest with 'City Dwellers', 'The Islandmen' – one of Rowley's most often quoted pieces, and in free verse too – 'The Clerk,' 'The Stitcher', 'A Gas Engine', and 'In a Tram'. *Workers* (1923) gathered some of these with a few other related poems such as 'Oul' Jane', and 'Machinery', illustrating them with woodcuts by E. M. O'Rorke Dickey (1894–1977). But it is in a more miscellaneous book of verse, *The Old Gods* (1925), that he makes the argument for his aspiration most explicit, in a blank verse poem, 'The Audience'. In this he declares that Beauty, for the poet

                    . . . shall walk
The common streets viewed by the enfranchised eyes
Of toiling men. . .
. . . it shall rise in the marketplace
Wide open to the city's traffic, wide
To all who pause from toil to enter in.
Here find your audience! The clattering mill
Shall hush to hark your song. The sounding steel
Shall still its clangour, and the shipyard hammers
Shall beat in rhythm to your melody
Through the abounding city, through the grime
Of smoke-encrusted walls, through streets unsunned. . .
In factories where palefaced women stoop
Tending the pitiless machines; amidst the steam
Of foundries where the molten metals hum. . .
. . . upon the windswept bridge
Thronged by the labour legions who return
Proud from their conquest over obdurate steel . . .

Thomas Carnduff (1880–1956) in his *Songs from the Shipyards* (1924) was obviously related to the same area of interest, and even a temporary resident, Patrick McDonogh (1902–1961) in his Belfast-printed *Leaf in the Wind* had one poem, 'A Belfast Shipping Clerk goes to his Work', which sets 'the bustle of the docks and shouting, shunts and whistles' against the pastoral quiet of County Wicklow. And when Carnduff, a little later, wrote his sub-O'Casey plays *Workers* (1932) and *Machinery* (1933) their titles were taken, their author admitted, from Rowley's verses.

Conor's paintings and drawings were obviously, it seemed, the visual counterpart of this literary activity, and he was, of course, an intimate friend of Rowley. But Carnduff – there is a fine drawing of him by Conor made for a volume which Rowley intended to publish from his Mourne Press in the early Forties – was already finding the industrial situation less romantic in his *Songs of an Out-of-work* (1932), and Rowley turned whole-heartedly to the countryside – he had kept his options open as early as 1924 with *County Down Songs*, illustrated by Lady Mabel Annesley (1881–1959) – Conor painted her portrait, too. Rowley's later books had such titles as *Ballads of Mourne* (1940) and *Sonnets for Felicity* (1942), far from gantry and factory floor. Carnduff's final play, *Castlereagh* (1935), backed well away into history.

So it appeared that Conor too had changed direction. This misconception lasted for years, until, on examining the collection of drawings and sketches in the Linen Hall Library in 1976, I chanced upon graphic notes made at country race meetings dated from the first decade of the century.

Leafing through the pencilled sheets, those which bore dates left no doubt of their period, and as my eye became adjusted to what I was coming to accept as his characteristic style of draughtsmanship, I came upon a drawing of a kitchen chair in a manner consistent with the rest. Asked to date it, I should have said 1910 or a year or two before that. But, on turning over the card on which the drawing had been made, I found that it was a printed invitation to the opening of an exhibition with the date 1956! So his draughtsmanship had hardly altered over the years.

Only in the more restricted field of portraiture can a shift in handling be observed. The half length of Rowley was carried out with abrupt strokes of a hogshair brush, with, in surface-texture if not in colour, a rather mosaic effect. It was this brusque brush-work, acceptable to a sophisticated friend, which I heard Conor declare made more conventional patrons reluctant to commission likenesses from him thereafter, demanding a more suave, flattering treatment – I think here of the painter in that Yeats poem who was able to 'smooth out stain and blemish with the elegance of his mind'. At any rate, when he painted Alderman J. A. Doran, Chairman of the Committee responsible for the Museum and Art Gallery, the pigment was thinner, the surface, though not slick, in no way agitated; with an admirable honesty, nothing of the aged man's rheumy eyes or claw-like talons was lost – I recollect that seeing this portrait once on a visit to Belfast, Dr. T. J. Honeyman, the Director of the Glasgow Art Gallery, a man with a well-schooled eye, commended it highly.

79. *Alderman J. A. Doran, J.P.*
1930. Oil on canvas.
74.6 × 62.4 cms sight
Ulster Museum Collection, Belfast.

Apart from this conscious change, it must be said that Conor evinced little technical curiosity, quite unlike several of the younger painters I have known. The greasy, sometimes scraped, drawings bear some relation to the drawings on stone he must have made when he worked at lithography at Allen's. Indeed his early training must have done much to determine his graphic methods. In later years, when confronted with the problem of painting his large 'mural' in the Museum, he certainly was at some pains to discover a way to keep his pigment matt, unreflecting, for on its destined wall it was to be subject to a raking side-light. He was proud then to declare that the 'Marble-medium', his term for whatever it was, would do the trick.

80. *At the Pump.*
N.d. Wax crayon on paper.
48.3 × 38.1 cms
Private collection.
Conor did a version of this picture in reverse which is in the Ulster Folk Museum Collection and was reproduced as a colour poster by the Arts Council of Northern Ireland in 1979.

## 3

It can be argued that with his visual vocabulary established in Edwardian days, he used his hoard of sketches to provide figures and details as suggestions for use in subsequent compositions. Broadly the clothes of his dwellers in the little streets seem to place them in some sharply imagined period in the past, although the actual paintings may have come decades later. For he usually avoided any close reference to fashion and the changes thereof, and generally took minimal note of the swift and striking changes in street furniture or vehicular traffic. His wartime drawing of the tramcar in the bomb-shattered terminus appears to be deeply indebted to a newspaper photograph.

This disregard for instantaneous contemporarity is not in itself any cause for adverse comment. The industrial landscapes of L. S. Lowry are peopled with heavily booted figures from some similar epoch in their painter's life, though Lowry, as a rent-collector for many years, must have been daily aware of the changes around him.

But the human moments remain valid out of time. Baudelaire had his lines for this phenomenon:

La forme d'une ville
Change plus vite, hélas, que le coeur d'un mortel.


## 4

Conor was no intellectual, no aesthetician. He seems never to have been tempted by whim or fashion into a decisive change of stylistic direction so typical of artists of this century. We have our own local examples of painters highly sensitive to the cultural barometer, the artistic seismograph of this volatile explosive epoch. Colin Middleton springs at once to mind, for he has applied wide-ranging talents to a multiplicity of styles – his first one man show in 1943 caused Thomas Carr to hail it as an anthology of modern art. He has experimented in and practised to mastery a variety from the non-objective and the abstracted to the surrealist, moving between these poles through innumerable degrees of representation. Even so single-minded an artist as John Luke (1906–1975) could just once produce his eccentric *Natas* (1935) in his progress from the topographical accuracy of *Connswater* (1934) to the soaring forms of *Northern Rhythms* (1943). Nor need the circumstance of Conor's remaining at home so consistently have cut him off in his backwater. Till Middleton's last decade neither he nor Luke had travelled as far as the older man. I have known one young artist deeply influenced by nothing more substantial than a magazine reproduction of an Edvard Munch and turn that experience to legitimate and lasting use in his development.

But though Conor was remarkably consistent in maintaining his own way of observing and recreating his material, he cannot be given any very useful or precise stylistic label more exact than Post-Impressionist. For this is a supremely elastic term, as the highly popular exhibition at the Royal Academy early in 1980 showed. This comprehensive display was assembled from countries as far apart as Canada and Switzerland, and included work by artists whose birthdates ranged from 1830 (Pissarro) to 1891 (Stanley Spencer). Into that elastic net Conor could fairly have fallen had the selectors known more about Irish painters and not shown such predilection for the Breton peasantry.

It is worth remarking that Holbrook Jackson in *The Studio* in 1925, wrote 'If one were tempted to pigeon hole William Conor one might say that he was the Manet of Belfast, particularly the Manet of *Le Bon Bock*.' But Jackson, whose proper field was Literature, did have the discrimination to add, 'This, however, applies only to form; in technique and in colour-sense he is powerfully and admirably himself'. Of Conor's colour-sense it would be fair to say that it appears normally harmonious if restricted.

Since the variety of Middleton's work is so great, over the years critics here offered scores of names of artists whom they can think of as likely influences upon him. But with Conor I have found a single reference to Steinlen in a French critical comment, and one to Daumier in Kenneth Jamison's essay on Painting and Sculpture in *Causeway* (1971), when he wrote: 'He is, perhaps, a kind of Irish Daumier, but without the bitter satirical edge; certainly an impressionist of sorts'.

5

Conor's lack of intellectual rigour is clear in his failure to organise his larger canvasses. With his *Opening of the Northern Ireland Parliament*, the sad story which Judith Wilson tells records plainly some of the hazards of this kind of commission; but, even allowing for these, the result is no way so entertaining as the *Proclamation of King Edward VII* (City Hall) begun by E. E. Taylor and finished by W. G. MacKenzie, with its serried rows of once recognisable big-wigs facing the anonymous backs of a vigorously cheering mob of obvious groundlings.

That 'mural' in Marble-medium already mentioned, the wall covering *Ulster Past and Present* commissioned by Sir Robert Baird, owner of the *Belfast Evening Telegraph*, was only marginally more successful. Baird was never reckoned among local patrons or supporters of the Arts, and was persuaded into this venture by Arthur Deane, the Curator of the Museum and Art Gallery, who, with his wife Grace, was among Conor's staunchest supporters. But values change, and long after the ceremonial unveiling of what was described in the programme rather surprisingly as 'a Fresco', hanging with some appropriateness in the archaeological room, it has, in recent years, been demoted, Sir Robert and the Curator safely dead, downstairs to a dark wall above the engines and textile machines of the Industrial section of the Ulster Museum.

The very title conveys more than a hint of the artist's or his sponsors' paucity of verbal imagination. In this huge canvas the left-hand side is crowded with a receding flow of legendary ancient Irish warriors in costumes which must have some relationship to the designs which the artist made for the St Patrick Pageant in 1932. These bronze-age or iron-

81. *The Jaunting Car.*
1933 approx. Oil on canvas.
70.5 × 90.5 cms sight
Ulster Museum Collection,
Belfast.

age veterans can be seen trudging past the centre-piece, a famous dolmen, and are balanced on the right by an approaching straggle of millgirls and male factory or shipyard workers passing the viewer to the extreme right – each apparently plucked separately from the artist's assembled sketches – one girl, her head hung in grief or deep thought, at once sets the viewer pondering on her particular past – and, above and behind them, a light background of clouds, gantries and mill chimneys.

I can remember very well that when the original cartoon had been completed, it had to be enlarged and transferred to the canvas. Conor, however, found that he could not unroll the canvas for this to be done, in the restricted confines of his Wellington Place studio. A lantern slide of the drawing was made. Brought from the studio to the Museum, the canvas was fully unfurled and propped in front of the film screen in the lecture hall. The slide was then projected and focused upon it and the outlines of the dolmen and the accompanying figures traced by the artist. It was rolled-up when this was done and taken back to the studio; Conor then painted it in handy sections as each was revealed, and rolled again when dry.

In smaller works than this, the picture-space often tends to become complicated, congested, making its organisation difficult. Crowded street scenes or crowded companies, as for example, seated and standing passengers in a tramcar or in a cinema queue, seldom offer any coherent design; each observed figure tends stubbornly to be separate. But he was much more effective in his compositions of single figures or small groups. Indeed it was with themes based on mother and child, a brace of travelling people, or a knot of gossiping neighbours that he most often achieved success in a unified composition. People on a tramcar, walking along the street, waiting for the train, are gathered by the chance of the occasion; where two or three are gathered together they communicate with each other; and that communication is the subject.

But whatever his subject figures were doing or wherever they were placed, there was always the danger of a muffed transition of gesture or articulation of limb. Hard hats or cloth caps do not invariably fit the heads they belong to. Crossed legs or legs in motion frequently gave him trouble, as with the young man in *Courtin'* (Ulster Museum) with one leg shorter than the other, or in *The Twelfth* (Ulster Folk Museum) in which we have some difficulty in associating legs with torsos; or there might be failure to communicate the bulk and volume of bodies or objects within the picture-space, as in *The Jaunting Car* (Ulster Museum) where the huddle of seated passengers is effectively posed in a pyramid, but the body of the horse seems unduly foreshortened or lost, taking up no space between the shafts. Even in so direct a statement as *The Elder Sister* – or 'Going to First Confession', as a friend suggests it might be called – from my own small collection, the left forearm of the protective girl, laid on the little boy's shoulder, has crumpled or collapsed into a mere suggestion of boneless fabric; the head of the girl is modelled, the boy's head in profile is two-dimensional. Physical substantiality too often eludes him. Among his drawings only one, known to me from a reproduction in a book, because of its boldly indicated contours, attains any exceptional presence, reminiscent a little of drawings by Mark Gertler or Bernard Meninisky; it certainly has that period look.

His rather naive attitude to matters relating to physical structure was made apparent to me quite by chance, when, one morning in 1931 or 1932, on the bus from the Cavehill Road into town, I occupied a seat just in front of Conor and an acquaintance – my memory insists that it was little Newton Penprase. In his talk William remarked – I could not avoid overhearing – that Tom Walmesley, Professor Walmesley of the Anatomy Department of the University, had, a day or two previously, invited him to visit the laboratory to see the work he was doing with the medical students. But he had declined, for, as he said firmly, 'I know enough about anatomy'. The irony of this was that Penprase was revered in the Art College for his encyclopaedic knowledge of anatomy, perspective, and all that goes with the finer points of perception.

6

Quality in art, as in all else, is very difficult if not impossible to define, so much depends on the variables of time, economic order, class, dress, fashion and the subjective taste and experience of the observer.

Anything I may have read on aesthetics has usually in the end compounded my confusion, or has, at best, nominated only temporary labels for isolated effects. 'Significant form', 'tactile values', 'architectural form' 'fitness for function' had at various times an ephemeral force.

After a lifetime's looking, while labels have withered in my mind, I have found temporary equilibrium in seeking for and laying my sensitivities open to what I now term the artist's Intensity and his Invention. But these possibilities are just as intractable to definition as any other; their frontiers shift and can interpenetrate or overlap.

By Intensity I mean, as fairly as I can phrase it, intensity of emotion, of sensory response, of observation, of realisation and representation of form and colour and texture, of line and shape, achievement of sensitive equilibrium. When applied the term may focus on one or any number of these kinds, and even then to varying degrees. The word Tension suggested itself to me, but I rapidly saw that it proved no alternative. Tension has two poles. Intensity, which includes it, gives the necessary

82. *The Elder Sister*.
1920 approx. Oil on canvas on board.
60 × 49.8 cms
Dr John Hewitt.

117

added direction; there can be tension *between* parts, but intensity is *of* something, a unified force. The other day I came upon some words by a neglected Victorian critic, J. Ashcroft Noble, which nudged my thought towards a closer definition of this quality as being 'generated by impassioned vision of a vividly apprehended reality'.

As examples of Intensity I could quote a still life with apples and pots by Cézanne, an interior by Vermeer, a group of male figures by Masaccio, a naked girl seated on a bed by Munch, a row of bottles by Morandi, harvesters asleep by Bruegel, a ravished saint by Bernini.

A friend skilled in assessing creative prose would substitute for Intensity the word Obsession. I find some value in it, but it is unfortunately an ambiguous term, teetering on the rims of sanity, so it might serve for Van Gogh, for Blake, for Bacon, for Munch, for Mondrian.

Invention has to do with organisation, design, resolution of formal problems, rhythm, elaboration of imaginative idea – here my two terms come very close together; I can appreciate but possess, as yet, no proper syntax by which I might define their oscillating frontier. Let me say that for Invention I could quote a painting by Poussin, a page of the Book of Kells, or a vegetable head by Arcimboldi.

## 7

Conor had little invention in organisation of his forms, succeeding only with the simplest arrangements, and for inventive imagination or even the cruder extensions of fantasy he had no facility or use. In design he relied upon the most obvious geometry, frequently on the diagonal, less frequently on the interplay of diagonals. He seldom seems to abstract from or impose upon the disparate parts of his assembled shapes any compulsive emblematically significant rhythm. Yet now and then within these limitations he can make evident his own kind of intensity, of life-enhancing emotion. It is human sympathy, affection, joy, humour, which he communicates. Pity, even pathos, but never tragedy, deep grief; never the mystic's exaltation, ecstasy or trance, or the satirist's searing scorn – the comment I have already quoted from Kenneth Jamison phrases this well.

The more readily shared moods and emotions which comprised his expressive lexicon are sufficiently pervasive not to be distanced by being as it were phrased in a slightly old-fashioned idiom; it is the outer semblance not the inner heart which changes.

## 8

His parents both survived beyond the accepted span. When they died, Conor was over fifty years of age. Freud has said somewhere that no man is truly adult until his father dies. If there should be truth in this it is likely that this parent-child relationship was, in some unconscious way, responsible for Conor's genuine vagueness about his actual age. The date of his birth shifted and was only established at the end of his life.

I can recall, in the Thirties, that Deane, introducing Conor's work to visitors from across the Irish Sea, would refer to him as a young artist.

Later I became a little amused as about that time I had noticed that Conor dyed his hair, not expertly, but as someone suggested, with his paint brush. I could not just then have guessed his age with any precision. The earliest watercolours in the Gallery's collection were a couple of dated military studies from the Great War years, and I did not know whether he had been an early or late beginner.

Insignificant as these recollections may appear, it could well be that, consciously or not, Conor was caught within this *persona* of sonship, in this myth of the young artist. This was not as absurd or reprehensible as it might seem; it was, we could say, poetically true, when we consider whence the springs of his most characteristic work were drawn. As artist he was born in the first decades of the century. It was not through simple filial piety that his own favourite among his paintings was the portrait of his mother.

83. *The Joke.*
Crayon drawing. Reproduced from *The Tree* published by the Ulster Society for the Prevention of Cruelty to Animals, Belfast, 1936.

Conor was unique among the artists of this country and this century. He was his own man. I can name no obvious local predecessor. He fathered no school of imitators, rallied no disciples to build doctrine and practice on his work. James Humbert Craig (1878–1944) established a kind of vision for and a manner of recording our Irish landscape which had its precursers but which he modified and developed to his own purpose, and thereafter found a crowd of imitators, his influence and rapid ascent to popularity so persistent that now, nearly forty years after his death, there are still picture-makers who long have turned his typical perceptions into tedious clichés.

Colin Middleton, that man of many intensities, surely our most accomplished and versatile painter, has always held Conor in high regard. For a very brief period Middleton found subjects in Belfast working class areas, depicting now and then a man pushing a handcart, a shawled girl singing outside a public house, children clustered round an ice-cream cart or hunkered at the kerb. But in this phase, in the early Forties, these were in no sense Conor pastiches. The colour range was richer, more various than lay on that artist's palette. The emphasis was on the streets themselves, the little red-brick rows, the painted doors and window frames; and these were often topographic, identified, as in *Nelson Street, Mary Street, Glenard* – a detail Conor never supplied. Their mood was elegiac, as if the artist were, in those threatening years, clutching and holding on to a moment at its most vulnerable. Comparing the rôle of figures in Middleton's streets with Conor's in their less emphatically realised backgrounds, I wrote in an essay on Middleton (1976): 'Colin's figures if present, were always firmly integrated in the townscape. William Conor's figures loomed largely caught in some posture which established the subject which normally had some sentimental point, often indicated by the title'.

Dan O'Neill (1920–1974) in one painting, *Birth* (Arts Council of Northern Ireland), unique among his romantic-expressionist variety, gave us a glimpse of Belfast working class life. But we can hardly imagine Conor attempting such a subject with the mother in the metal bed, the aproned friend holding the swaddled child, the shirt-sleeved doctor closing his bag, and the small boy gazing in fascination at the kettle, the large bottle and the liquid-filled bowl on the table. This has a tension, a wry watchfulness and a deep wonder, which no one would mistake for the work of any other artist.

Another Belfast-born painter, Gerard Dillon (1916–1971), might come to mind, for he was familiar with and recreated some aspects of the life and environment of common people in his native city. Among his earliest paintings I recall those of the bomb-shattered streets of the war years. Stylistically he worked so strongly within the territory marked out by the Englishman Christopher Wood, and found his particular lonely pathos and innocent pieties more easily in rocky Connemara and the Irish Romanesque, that he can scarcely be considered to have given more than a brief and distant salutation to our man, though in temperament I believe them to have had much in common, the compassion, the charity, the rapport, the innate shyness.

Perhaps it was Conor's pointing of the way which prompted Padraig Marrinan (1906–1972) to use Belfast figures and themes; but in brushwork and colour utilised in a general naiveté of vision edging towards the caricatural, utterly at odds with Conor's affectionate eye, these could only be claimed remotely as derivative.

One other artist could be mentioned here, Liam Andrews, born 1913, who, although he attended the School of Art, remained resolutely isolated in his own territory of West Belfast. Indeed, his first comprehensive exhibition was held in November 1980 in the Andersonstown Leisure Centre. An avowed admirer of Conor, he has made the representation of the people and the streets of his chosen area his principal subject matter. But by now, shedding all but the merest hint of the older artist's manner, his water colours successfully evoke the interaction of people and places.

## 10

When Conor's idiosyncratic figures find themselves brought together in a drawing or painting, it is as if the spectator, the observer, were eavesdropping, overhearing some snatch of conversation, some tatter of gossip, badinage, rumour or song, some brief word of greeting, of endearment or comfort. Those figures which are silent are about to speak. Someone is paying attention, listening, even if it is only the pacified infant.

But trapped in this web of social intercourse, we can have little regard or any heed for abstract formulations. We are no analysts of form, line or colour. We are seldom made aware of texture. The meaning lies beyond these; it belongs to human behaviour, physically within the compass and context of the particular instant in time, but so fundamental that the factors are subsumed in the event.

Here we approach some sort of distinction, definition. These pictures belong to romantic art, generous in feeling, humble, basic, a low-keyed romanticism, intense in its kind; for this is the stuff of ordinary life, the everyday plains and level lands of living, not the challenging ascents, harsh declivities, or lonely peaks of experience, with ground level not rarefied air. They leak out in normality. This selector and recorder of daily existence is no symphonic architect. The tilt is towards literature, not music. When his people sing it is a common song, no abstract aria. The other kind of picture is self-contained, exists entirely within its frame.

Yet in literary terms these are anecdotal, not epic. And it is well to remember that, as Brian Fallon wrote in the *Irish Times* (24 May 1980), reviewing a biography of William Mulready, an Irishman but expatriate, 'Many critics have never forgiven him for being anecdotal, but after all, most of the Dutch Old Masters painted anecdotes, and an anecdote or incident is as legitimate a starting point for a picture as is a still life or nude; it is the result that should be judged'. There are, of course, risks with the anecdote; it may be trivial, without much point, or disturbingly sentimental. Conor sometimes falls into that trap, but his occasions, confrontations, usually make their point, and in his abundant concern for his folk, that point had often the resonance of the best of all anecdotes, the parable.


## 11

I have in these foregoing paragraphs attempted to find words for my responses to the kind of work most of us associate with the name of Conor, and that has not been without some difficulty, for the contemporary critical jargon is a pallid, opaque, inflexible, pseudo-cerebral exercise, ill-adapted to vibrate to sensory or emotional stimuli.

My reactions to the common humanity in his works has not, by any means, diverted me from other elements he has been able to present. And when I think back over the many paintings of his not merely to be corralled in categories for the purposes of this survey but as individual items which I associate with his name which have been instant and lasting sources of pleasure and delight, those which memory plucks out, casually, not in any order of merit, are these. First that painting, called, when the American company bought it, *Irish Horse Parade*, appropriate enough, although I have always thought of it as *The Farmers' Race*. I have not seen it for nearly fifty years, but I remember it vividly. And just as vividly I recollect the circumstances of its American purchase.

About 1934 the British representative of the firm – we would call it a multinational nowadays – had been asked by Head Office to find two pictures to demonstrate the quality of Northern Irish painters in the big international collection they were forming. He approached Arthur Deane as a responsible judge. Deane naturally thought of Conor his friend, and when this picture came in I was highly pleased, and because I agreed with him so wholeheartedly he allowed me to propose a John Luke landscape as our number two. Told like this, it sounds a piece of horse-trading, but these were in fact two commendable paintings, as good as could be found in the Six Counties at that time.

The detail in this painting which comes first to mind is the back view of the farmer standing in the righthand foreground, the dividing diagonal of the string of fence-posts framing the spectators in a right angle triangle, and the zig-zag of the pacing horses from the top left hand down and across, along the posts. Here the design is more complicated than usual; the customary diagonal, the zig-zag, the triangle, the static watchers and the continuous passing of the horses and the striding men, stillness and movement.

I remember too, from seeing it first at that Guild exhibition in Arthur Square, the comely half-length nude of the coloured girl, so far outside the Conor canon – she must have been the model Paul Henry introduced him to, in London, the girl who, when William announced his intention of going back to Belfast, wanted to come with him. Imagine the alarm and consternation in Landscape Terrace!

Then there was the small oil of the huntsman in the red jacket trotting his horse along the Lagan towpath, brilliant against the leafy trees –

84. *City Hall Under Snow.*
N.d. Oil on canvas on board.
42.9 × 53.3 cms
Ulster Museum Collection,
Belfast.

where did I see this? In Tyrone House, Ormeau Avenue or 55A Donegall Place? It was bought by Dr Nesca Robb, that shy, plump scholar.

Two more perhaps, the larger canvas of the great red and white bull buoyant with energy, passing through the cattle show like a monarch. I saw this first in the studio on the Stranmillis Road when we were sorting out pieces for the retrospective of 1957. And in the same exhibition, but, I remember, on loan from Dublin, the smallish head of Lynn Doyle, painted with prismatic knife strokes, with a vivacity and sparkle none of the other portraits of his friends possessed. My memory may be playing me false, may be flattering the actual canvasses. I have no way of reassessing or confirming my first judgments; but on the occasions when I first saw them I felt that each had quality, some measure of what I shall now call intensity, and, in retrospect, they have remained with me, what Constable would have called, 'additions to my estate'.

When I think of these memorable works and others with which I have been more familiar, the portraits of old Alderman Doran and of the artist's mother, the cool and sombre *City Hall Under Snow* as seen from his Wellington Place studio, and the watercolours of Armagh, Downpatrick and the ferry boats on the Lagan, I find it exceedingly difficult to reconcile one who appears to have been a highly professional painter of considerable resource with the sometimes kindly, clumsy, sentimental, often banal artist to whom nothing in the daily life of the people of his youth was alien, who could conjure out of the general drabness the warm glow of life.

## 12

This could well prompt me to wonder about the direction Conor might have taken had he found it possible to settle in London when he first made the attempt. Would the evident skill and the expanding curiosity which seems to emerge from these non-canonical works have been applied to a much greater extent, susceptible to and modified by the trends and tendencies then so influential at the metropolitan centre? Would his technique have matured in some unanticipated direction, so that he might have secured a firm footing among the better known artists where, to use Kenneth Clark's words, 'standards of skill are higher and patrons more exacting'? But should we then have lost entirely the home-rooted Conor and those works which grew out of that rootedness?

Yet, socially unsure of himself, vulnerable, threatened, he felt, by metropolitan pressures, it seems that he could do no other than retreat to the safety of his family home. This family which long remained intact to a remarkable degree through all its changes of address – which, in fact, did not range more than a street or two – provided a basis and location of support and sympathy, through and within which he had ready access to the deep reservoir of images, sensations and experiences of working class life, determined by the robust ideology of that class, with its albeit communal values already given a visual code by his indefatigable note-taking and sketching in the markets, streets and alleys of his earlier years.

## 13

Conor was greatly irked by the frequency and unanimity with which he was categorised as the painter of Belfast working class life, for he believed it unjust, limiting, ignoring his treatment of other subjects for his skill which could have been more popular with potential patrons. He much preferred to be known in comprehensive terms as 'portraitist, landscapist and genre painter', as he was described in one catalogue note which bears every sign of having been composed by a close friend with his prompting and approval.

But in the first of these departments he never really became a leading practitioner, nationally or locally. Dublin was, of course, the capital of the country until partition, besides being the home ground of the Royal Hibernian Academy. So in the field of portraiture it has been abundantly serviced. The long established figures were Sarah Purser (1848–1943), Dermot O'Brien (1865–1945), President of the RHA from 1910 to his death, Sarah C. Harrison (c1864–1941) who had come to Dublin in the 1880s from her home in Co Down. The powerful presence of William Orpen (1878–1931) propelled a vigorous generation. Patrick Tuohy (1894–1930), Leo Whelan (1892–1956), Margaret Clarke

(1888–1961), Estelle Solomons (1882–1968), pupils of Orpen, were Conor's contemporaries, as was his fellow Ulsterman James Sleator (1889–1950), who had come from Armagh in 1910.

These were joined or followed, in Conor's middle years, by the popular Sean O'Sullivan (1906–1964) and Hilda Roberts (born 1901) who had been a pupil of Tuohy. With all these plying their craft in acceptable varieties of portraiture there was little room for any less facile brush. Though Conor occasionally painted Dublin friends, it was not until the presentation portrait of Douglas Hyde that he penetrated this market.

At home in the Belfast of his earlier years the most prestigious commissions were monopolised by an Englishwoman, Henrietta Rae, who regularly visited the town, renting a studio each time. W. G. MacKenzie (1859–1924) was nearing the end of his career and turning more and more to landscape. Harry R. Douglas, painstakingly pedestrian, realised his peak achievement in a wide painting of Sir Robert Meyer, Town Clerk, caught at his capacious desk behind a monumental telephone and a rack of City Hall notepaper.

In the Spring of 1927 the Belfast Art Gallery organised an Exhibition of Irish Portraits which we may take as not unfairly representative of the period. From the catalogue we can see that of locally-born artists then living, Miss Harrison led with seven works, followed by David Bond Walker and W. Arthur Fry with four each. Douglas and Sleator had two apiece. Frank McKelvey, an Associate of the RHA for four years, had many exhibits, but nearly all were pencil and wash copies of nineteenth century originals and so lie outside our concern. Conor was represented by his portrait of a son of Richard Hayward, already mentioned in Judith Wilson's narrative; Hayward himself had trusted his likeness to Bond Walker. So it may be taken that Conor, now forty-six – for most artists, about their prime – had not so far found any notable position among local portrait painters.

In landscape, J. W. Carey had long been popular for his modestly priced watercolours of the Mourne country and the Co Down coast, in a style which had survived from well back in the last century. James Humbert Craig, from about 1920, was asserting his extension of Paul Henry's manner, a modified manner which was to become the stable convention for generations. McKelvey was refurbishing the MacKenzie style with a brighter palette. Conor, although successful with his few harbour watercolours, could not compete with any of these in popular appeal. Indeed, his later oil landscapes, several of them of the Lagan, employed compositions perhaps derived from the memory of play-posters or stage designs. These tended to have a flat, two-dimensional effect, using a framework of leaning trees and overhanging branches to enclose a centre-void of placid water, as if leaving space for absent actors, or lettering, to occupy. It is surprising that none of his surviving works shows any trace of his old teacher at the Art School, George Trobridge (1851–1909), whose influence persisted in other pupils' work, in some instances, until the late Thirties. With such competition in both portrait and landscape, it was obvious that Conor's working class studies alone gave him a unique place among local artists.

In Ireland there had long been a tradition in using romantic rural themes, the country fair, the faction fight, saints' patron festivities, which pictorially were consistent with the popular stage-Irish myth, when already in France by mid-century Millet had presented his peasants with affection and dignity, relating them to their daily tasks, not to horseplay and buffoonery. But Jack B. Yeats (1871–1957) in his lively illustrations for *Life in the West of Ireland* (1912) – and other books – gave a new and more authentic particularisation of village types far from the Erskine Nicholl stereotypes or the coarse distortions of the English cartoonists.

Just at the same time (1912) Paul Henry found Achill potato diggers, fishermen, turf workers, old folk watching a country dance and similar material fit to render in a way which he had learned from seeing his first Van Goghs. His first exhibition took place in Belfast in 1913; and it could have been this which woke Conor to the possibility of drawing on that hoard of sketches which he had made and was continuing to make, of his own humble townsfolk as subjects for more elaborate treatment with oil colours or coloured crayons, thereby becoming pioneer in this kind of work in Ireland.


## 14

When, in *Art in Ulster I* (1977), I designated Conor as 'a proletarian artist without protest', at the back of my mind lay some muffled reference to that other tradition which Millet had begun of giving realistic respect to country labour, after the era of the rococo sylvan idylls. Millet's works, *The Gleaners*, *The Sower*, *The Angelus*, *The Man with the Hoe*, became, through popular reproductions, internationally famous. Their high example offered painters in many countries a new range of legitimate subjects, and it was not long before some of them began to treat urban figure subjects with a serious regard, since Millet's passionate belief in democratic and socialist ideals gave an ironic significance to, and a set of symbols for, the dignity of labour and the worth of the common man.

In Britain this new interest won its way into the pages of the popular magazines the *Graphic* and the *Illustrated London News*, which began to carry fine wood engravings after drawings by artists such as Frank Holl, Luke Fildes, Hubert Herkomer, of workers and workless, of the destitute, the poorhouse queues, of the new vast industrial cities. These were presented with honesty, with pity for the haggard wife and the hungry children, the patient suppliants at the soup-kitchen door. But it was a qualified pity, consonant with accepted social values, for the simply unfortunate, the victims of an inexorable fate, rather than the exploited, the dispossessed of a harsh acquisitive society.

To respond to these, more passionate reactions became characteristic of artists in some Continental countries where industrialisation was more recent and more raw, and class antagonisms much sharper. By the century's end in Germany perhaps the first of these artists of discontent was Kathe Kollwitz (1867–1945). Unfortunately her graphic work is little known in these islands, but she has naturally a high reputation in the German Democratic Republic. Wife of a medical doctor working in a poor district in Berlin, she found her material among her husband's patients and in the neighbourhood of his practice, in slum pregnancies, strikes, demonstrations, and all the hardships of the poor.

Yet looking through a comprehensive book of her drawings, you could not help being struck by the similarity of many of them to work by Conor: the studies of mothers and children, the wide-eyed little girl, the work-weary artisan. Appreciate the bolder line, the firmer grasp of anatomy, these still could well be within Conor's range. Here is the same compassion, the same social respect, the same sympathy, but her studies of dead infants, battered strikers, sound a more strident note, a cry of outrage, a cry against injustice, a call for social change.

Yes; he is a proletarian artist without protest. But how could he have been other? In Great Britain where its citizens are conditioned to the Ins and the Outs, the alternations of governments and opposition, the seesaws of liberal democracy, there have been few artists with any highly activated or overt social conscience. Here in Northern Ireland where people have never experienced actual bread-and-butter politics, splashing as they do in the last subsiding ripples of the Thirty Years' War, he would have been false to his folk if he had attempted to insert that missing element in their archaic ideology, a realisation of the contradictions within a market economy. The tenor of his work generally was genial – kindly, sociable, are among the dictionary's meanings of the word. He never gave the slightest hint that he, at anytime, considered his people to be victims of, or conditioned by, the inevitable crises of a profit and loss society.


## 15

Kenneth Clark, in his presidential address to the English Association on *Provincialism* (1962), summed up 'the characteristics of a positive and independent provincial art: it tells a story: it takes pleasure in the facts; it is lyrical, and it achieves a visionary intensity'. We can, without discreditable manipulation, apply these specifics to Conor's art. His figures or groups of figures tell a story, though often no more than a very short one. He enjoys keeping to the prose facts of appearance and gesture, having no need for, or facility in, fantasy, or unanchored imagination. But this grip on the actual transcends the prosaic; each drawing or painting is, in its degree, lyrical; its song is of human existence, of motherhood, neighbourliness, companionship, simple labour. I should substitute the adjective 'affectionate' for 'visionary' in fixing on its intensity, for Conor never imagines more than he has proved on his pulses. So no one need be dismayed or deem that it is dismissive if Provincial should be taken as a just description of William Conor's characteristic art.

# Chronology

| | |
|---|---|
| 1881 | William Conor born 9 May at 5 Fortingale Street, Belfast, to William Connor and Mary (*née* Wallace). |
| 1884 | Family now living at 6 Fortingale Street. |
| 1887 | Family now living at 22 Fortingale Street. |
| 1888 | Began his education, aged 6, on 19 March at Clifton Park Central National School, Avoca Street, Belfast. |
| 1890 | Family now living at 51 Upper Glenfarne Street, Belfast. (House became No. 45 when street was renumbered in 1892.) |
| 1891 | Sat his first drawing examination. |
| 1894 | Began his art education at Belfast Government School of Art (renamed Municipal Technical Institute in 1902). |
| 1902 | Family now living at 40 Perth Street, Belfast. |
| 1903 | Became assistant teacher in Antique at the Municipal Technical Institute. |
| 1904 | Left the Institute and joined David Allen and Sons Ltd, a firm of lithographers. |
| 1906 | Family now living at 3 Landscape Terrace, Belfast. |
| 1907–09 | Occasionally signed his sketching notes as Liam, Liam Conor or Liam O'Conocohair. |
| 1909 | Older brother Hugh married and emigrated to Canada. |
| 1910 (approx) | Left Allens, lived for a while in a cottage at Craigavad, Co Down, stayed for a few months on the Great Blasket Island, Co Kerry. |
| 1910 | Works hung for the first time at the Belfast Art Society. |
| 1911–12 | Made sketching trips to Co Donegal, and possibly at this time spent six months in Paris. |
| 1912 | Eldest brother Matthew, with wife and year old son, emigrated to England. |
| 1913 | Elected a Member of the Committee on the Council of the Belfast Art Society. |
| 1914 | Appointed an Official War Artist. |
| 1916 | Exhibition of 33 war drawings were auctioned in aid of the Ulster Volunteer Force Patriotic Fund on 19 December. |
| 1917 | Elected one of four Vice-Presidents of the Belfast Art Society. |
| 1918 | Works hung for the first time in the Royal Hibernian Academy, Dublin. |
| 1918 | Black and white illustrations appeared in Lynn Doyle's *Ballygullion*, published by Maunsel, Dublin and London. |
| 1919 | Painted portrait of his mother. |
| 1921 | Stayed for a time in London at 32 Percy Street off the Tottenham Court Road where E. M. O'R. Dickey already had accommodation. |
| 1921 | Four works accepted at the Spring Exhibition of the London National Portrait Society. |
| 1921 | 30 works exhibited at the Dawson Gallery, Dublin. |
| 1921 | Painted the *Opening of the First Northern Ireland Parliament* (22 June). |
| 1921 | Obtained a studio at 7 Chichester Street, Belfast. |
| 1921 | Exhibited for the first time at the Royal Academy, London. |
| 1921 | Two works hung at the Société National des Beaux-Arts Salon de 1921. |

| 1921 | One work hung for the first time at the Royal Society of Portrait Painters, London. |
|---|---|
| 1921 | One work hung at the Exhibition of the International Society of Painters, Sculptors and Gravers. |
| 1921 | One work hung for the first time at the Royal Glasgow Institute of the Fine Arts 60th Annual Exhibition. |
| 1922 | Exhibition held at John Magee's Donegall Square West Gallery, Belfast. |
| 1922 | Work included in the Exhibition of Irish Artists held at the Gallerie Barbazanges, Paris. |
| 1922 | One work hung in the Colour Magazine Exhibition of Modern Art at the Grosvenor Gallery, London. (29 March–12 April. No. 10, *The Lost Child*, Oil, £50.) |
| 1922 | Work hung at the Société National des Beaux-Arts Salon de 1922. |
| 1922 | One work hung at the Royal Glasgow Institute of the Fine Arts. |
| 1922 | One work hung at the Grosvenor Gallery Annual Summer Exhibition, London. |
| 1922 | Three works hung during Nov/Dec at the Goupil Gallery, Salon Exhibition, London. |
| 1922 | One work hung at the Grosvenor Gallery Annual Winter Exhibition, London. |
| 1923 | Three works purchased by the Manchester City Art Gallery. |
| 1923 | The above three works shown at the Collectors Gallery, Manchester, then at the Goupil Gallery, London. |
| 1923 | 43 works hung at the Goupil Gallery, London. |
| 1923 | Exhibition held at John Magee's Gallery, Belfast. |
| 1923 | One work hung at the Goupil Gallery Salon Exhibition, London. |
| 1923 | Three works included in an exhibition of European Artists in Sydney, Australia. |
| 1924 | 45 works hung at the St Stephen's Green Gallery, Dublin. |
| 1924 | One work hung at the Royal Academy, London. |
| 1924 | One work hung at the Royal Society of Portrait Painters, London. |
| 1924 | One of the 18 artists whose work, which included *The Politician*, was exhibited at the Pollock Gallery of Paintings, 47 Donegall Place, Belfast, during August. |
| 1924 | Member of the Belfast Art Society Dramatic Club. |
| 1924 | Two works hung at the Goupil Gallery Salon Exhibition, London. |
| 1925 | Two works hung at the Royal Glasgow Institute of the Fine Arts. |
| 1925 | 50 works hung at the St Stephen's Green Gallery, Dublin. |
| 1925 | He gave up his studio at 7 Chichester Street, Belfast, at the end of this year due to his rooms having been let. |
| 1926 | Poster designed for the Tourist Development Association shown at railway stations throughout Great Britain. |
| 1926 | Elected one of four Vice-Presidents of the Belfast Art Society, |
| 1926 | On 26 June left aboard the Cunarder *Berengeria* for the Philadelphia Convention of the World's Advertising Club in America. |
| 1926 | Spent remainder of the summer with Reverend W. B. Lusk and family in Ridgefield, Connecticut. |
| 1926 | In October held an exhibition of 'Irish Life' in the Babcock Galleries, New York. |

| | |
|---|---|
| 1927 | Included in an exhibition of 'Water Colors, Paintings, Pastels and Drawings by American and European Artists' held at the Brooklyn Museum, New York. |
| 1927 | Exhibition of his work held in the premises of the American Irish Historical Society, New York. |
| 1927 | Two portraits painted during his stay: *Judge Richard Campbell* and *Reverend Father John H. Dooley*. |
| 1927 | Left America on 12 March aboard the S.S. *Asconia* for England. |
| 1927 | One work included in 'A Loan Exhibition of Irish Portraits by Ulster Artists' held during February at the Municipal Museum and Art Gallery, Belfast. |
| 1927 | Acquired a studio at 1 Wellington Place, Belfast. |
| 1927 | On 23 May during British Empire Week held an Empire Exhibition at his studio. |
| 1927 | One work hung at the Royal Academy, London. |
| 1927 | One of 8 artists included in an 'Exhibition of Water Colour Drawings and Paintings', in Grand Central Hotel, Belfast from 18 to 29 October. |
| 1927 | One work hung at the Exhibition of the Work of Living British Artists under the auspices of the British Artists' Exhibition at the Municipal Museum and Art Gallery, Belfast. |
| 1928 | Two works hung at the Exhibition of the Work of Living British Artists under the auspices of the British Artists' Exhibition at the Municipal Museum and Art Gallery, Plymouth. (25 February–14 April. No. 64, oil, *The Accompanist*, £31.10.0 and No. 147, in the water colour, drawing, etc., section *At the Docks*, £10.10.0.) |
| 1928 | One work hung at the Royal Society of Portrait Painters, London. |
| 1928 | One work hung at the 'Pictures with a Subject' exhibition held at the City of Manchester Queen's Park Art Gallery. |
| 1928 | Elected one of four Vice-Presidents of the Belfast Art Society. |
| 1928 | Invited to submit work to the Royal National Eisteddfod of Wales at Treorchy. |
| 1928 | One work hung at the Royal Glasgow Institute of the Fine Arts. |
| 1928 | Black and white illustration of *A Bit of a Tune* appeared in *An Ulster Garland* in aid of the Hospital for Sick Children (published by McCaw, Stevenson and Orr, Belfast). |
| 1929 | 45 works exhibited at the Godfrey Phillips Gallery, London. |
| 1929 | One work hung at the Exhibition of the Work of Living British Artists under the auspices of the British Artists' Exhibition at the Walker Art Gallery, Liverpool. |
| 1930 | Two works hung at the Royal Society of Portrait Painters, London. |
| 1930 | One work hung in a retrospective exhibition of works purchased during the previous three years at the British Artists' Exhibition held in the City Guild Hall, London. |
| 1930 | A founder member and one of the first nine Academicians when the Belfast Art Society became the Ulster Academy of Arts. |
| 1930 | Three works hung at the Royal Glasgow Institute of the Fine Arts. |
| 1930 | Elected a founder member of the National Society of Painters, Sculptors and Gravers, and exhibited four works in the 1st Annual Exhibition. |

| 1930 | Illustrated a series of six articles entitled 'Beauty in Ulster' for the *Daily Express*. |
|---|---|
| 1931 | Family now living at 62 Westland Road, Belfast. The house was listed in Conor's name as tenant. |
| 1931 | One work hung at the Royal Academy, London. |
| 1931 | Three works hung at the Royal Glasgow Institute of the Fine Arts. |
| 1931 | Exhibited at the National Society of Painters, Sculptors, and Gravers. |
| 1932 | Exhibited at the National Society of Painters, Sculptors, and Gravers. |
| 1932 | One work hung at the Royal Academy, London. |
| 1932 | Two works hung at the Royal Society of Portrait Painters, London. |
| 1932 | First Irishman to be elected a member of the Royal Institute of Oil Painters (ROI); showed four works in the Institute's annual exhibition. |
| 1932 | Designed costumes for Richard Rowley's *The Pageant of Saint Patrick*. |
| 1932 | Painted *Ulster Past and Present*. |
| 1932 | Two works hung at the Royal Glasgow Institute of the Fine Arts. |
| 1933 | One work hung at the Royal Society of Portrait Painters, London. |
| 1933 | Was a member of the Northern Ireland Guild of Artists formed in 1933; exhibited at the State Buildings, Arthur Square, Belfast. Guild disbanded soon after. |
| 1933 | Father died 29 August aged 84. |
| 1933 | One work hung at the Royal Glasgow Institute of the Fine Arts. |
| 1933 | Four works hung at the Royal Institute of Oil Painters, London. |
| 1933 | Mother died 13 December aged 81. |
| 1934 | One work hung at the Royal Society of Portrait Painters, London. |
| 1934 | Four works hung at the Royal Institute of Oil Painters, London. |
| 1934 | One work hung at the Royal Glasgow Institute of the Fine Arts. |
| 1935 | Wrote an open letter to the *Belfast Telegraph* warning the public about fakes purporting to be his work. |
| 1935 | The Thomas Haverty Trust purchased his set of 16 pastel costume designs for *The Pageant of Saint Patrick* and presented them to the Hugh Lane Gallery, Dublin. |
| 1935 | One work hung at the Royal Academy, London. |
| 1935 | One work hung at the Royal Society of Portrait Painters, London. |
| 1935 | Four works hung at the Royal Institute of Oil Painters, London. |
| 1935 | Three works hung at the Royal Glasgow Institute of the Fine Arts. |
| 1936 | Lent one of his works to the Bradford Corporation, England. |
| 1936 | Included in a Circulating Exhibition by the Art Exhibition Bureau, London. |
| 1936 | Stayed for a short time at the Chelsea Arts Club, London. |
| 1936 | While in London painted a portrait of Denys Lowson. |
| 1936 | Four works hung at the Royal Institute of Oil Painters, London. |
| 1936 | Two works hung at the Royal Glasgow Institute of the Fine Arts. |
| 1936 | Became an Honorary Academician of the Ulster Academy of Arts. |

| 1937 | Family now living at 107 Salisbury Avenue, Belfast. |
| 1937 | One work hung at the Royal Academy, London (*Strangford Lough, Co Down*, Conor's first large landscape). |
| 1937 | Painted a portrait of King George VI from studies made at a Garden Party at Stormont. |
| 1937 | Four works hung at the Royal Institute of Oil Painters, London. |
| 1937 | One work hung at the Royal Glasgow Institute of the Fine Arts. |
| 1938 | Lynn Doyle opened Conor's exhibition at Combridges Gallery, Dublin. |
| 1938 | Two works hung at the Royal Academy, London. |
| 1938 | Elected an Associate Member of the Royal Hibernian Academy, Dublin. |
| 1939 | Series, 'Drawing The Crowd', in the *Irish Times* (6 January 1940); No. 7 was a caricature of Conor by Alan Reeve drawn in 1939. |
| 1939 | Included in 'The Art of 79 Countries', an exhibition held by the International Business Machines Corporation at the New York World Fair. |
| 1939 | Two works hung at the Royal Academy, London. |
| 1939 | Two works hung at the Royal Glasgow Institute of the Fine Arts. |
| 1939 | Again made an Official War Artist. |
| 1940 | His picture *Building an Air Raid Shelter in a Belfast Street* included in the War Artists' Exhibition at the National Gallery, London. |
| 1940 | Exhibition of his war pictures opened at the Ulster Arcade (Brands) Ltd, in December during Belfast's War Weapons Week. |
| 1940 | Left his studio at 1 Wellington Place, Belfast, and gave his address as The Academy Club, 18 Brookhill Avenue, Belfast. |
| 1941 | Family stayed with their cousins the Misses Milliken in Carryduff, Co Down for a few months during the Blitz. |
| 1941 | His exhibition 'Air Raid Memories' opened in the Linen Salon of Robinson & Cleaver's, Belfast. |
| 1942 | The only artist permitted to record the landing of the first American troops in Northern Ireland on 26 January. |
| 1943 | One work hung at the Royal Glasgow Institute of the Fine Arts. |
| 1944 | Acquired a studio at 11a Stranmillis Road, Belfast. |
| 1944 | His book *The Irish Scene* published by Derrick MacCord, Belfast. |
| 1944 | CEMA Exhibition. |
| 1944 | Exhibition of his work held at the Waddington Galleries, Dublin, Nov/Dec. Three of his horse racing pictures on exhibition were used as cover illustrations for the *Irish Field* 23 December 1944. |
| 1945 | Designed dust jacket for Lynn Doyle's *A Bowl of Broth* (Duckworth, London). |
| 1945 | Royal Academy of Arts, London held an Exhibition of National War Pictures, from 13 Oct to 25 Nov, including Conor's *Building an Air Raid Shelter in a Belfast Street*. |
| 1945/46 | CEMA held an exhibition of 30 of his works in Tyrone House, Belfast; this then became the first of a series of one man shows to tour the Province. |
| 1946 | Employees of Ulster Carpet Mills Ltd, Portadown, commissioned Conor to paint the portrait of the firm's founder, George Walter Wilson. |

| | |
|---|---|
| 1947 | Included in the CEMA Exhibition of Ulster Painters, held for the opening of the Government of Northern Ireland's new offices in London. |
| 1947 | Designed dust jacket for Lynn Doyle's *Green Oranges* published by Duckworths, London. |
| 1947 | Canadian firm, Messrs Cook of Toronto, produced a brochure and advertising cards for a promotional scheme, using five of Conor's crayon drawings. |
| 1947 | Elected a full member of the Royal Hibernian Academy, Dublin. |
| 1948 | Exhibition held at the Waddington Galleries, Dublin. |
| 1950 | Designed the dust jacket and illustrated John Irvine's *By Winding Roads* (H. R. Carter Publications, Belfast). |
| 1950 | CEMA exhibition of his work in their Donegall Place Gallery, Belfast. |
| 1951 | Works by Conor from the Zoltan Lewinter Frankl Collection included in an exhibition of 'Contemporary Ulster Painting' held by the Scottish Committee of the Arts Council in Edinburgh. |
| 1951 | Received invitation to Festival of Britain Dedication at St Paul's Cathedral, London. |
| 1951 | During Bangor Civic Week 30 June to 7 July, an exhibition of paintings loaned by Bangor residents was held in the Guild Hall. No. 97 *Study of a Child* by Conor was lent by Mr T. Drummond. |
| 1952 | Awarded the O.B.E. |
| 1952 | Brother Martin died on 3 August. |
| 1953 | Brother John died on 13 March. |
| 1956 | Designed the dust jacket for Lynn Doyle's *The Ballygullion Bus* (Duckworth, London). |
| 1957 | Retrospective exhibition of 151 works by Conor held by CEMA, at the Museum and Art Gallery, Belfast. |
| 1957 | Awarded an Honorary Degree of Master of Arts from the Queen's University of Belfast. Elected President RUA. |
| 1958 | Sister Mary died on 18 April. |
| 1959 | Granted a Civil List pension by the Minister of Finance, Captain Terence O'Neill, on behalf of the Government of Northern Ireland. |
| 1959 | Served on the Jury to select the winner of the Royal Institute of British Architects' Bronze Medal. |
| 1959 | Gave up his studio at 11a Stranmillis Road, Belfast, to work from his home, 107 Salisbury Avenue. |
| 1962 | Works included in an Exhibition presented by CEMA in association with Dungannon Urban and Rural District Council held in the Royal School, Dungannon. |
| 1963 | Works included in an Ulster Arts Club exhibition held in the Ulster Museum. |
| 1964 | The Royal Ulster Academy held a dinner at the Wellington Park Hotel, Belfast on the occasion of Conor's retirement as their President. Nine of his pictures were hung. |
| 1964 | Conor lent a portfolio of his work to Ulster Television to illustrate a series of programmes entitled 'The Humour is on me Now'. |
| 1964 | Exhibition of 41 Conor pictures opened at the Bell Gallery, Belfast. |

| 1965 | Included in a representative exhibition of Ulster Art staged in Selfridges Gallery, London. |
|------|---|
| 1965 | Exhibition held in the Art room of Victoria College, Belfast. |
| 1965 | Donated one work to the Memorial Fund Exhibition for Sam Thompson held in the Bell Gallery. |
| 1965 | Two works included in the 'Exhibition of Great Irishmen' held at the Ulster Museum. |
| 1965 | Exhibition of work opened at the Botanic Inn, Belfast, in December. |
| 1966 | Seventy-seven works exhibited in 'Belfast of Yesterday' held at the Bell Gallery, Belfast, in February. |
| 1966 | His 85th birthday celebrations held in the City Hall, Belfast. |
| 1966 | Three works included in an exhibition of selected pictures and sculptures from the W. A. N. MacGeough Bond collection. |
| 1967 | Thirty-eight works included in Conor exhibition at the Bell Gallery, Belfast. |
| 1968 | Took part in 'To-day and Yesterday in Northern Ireland', a BBC radio series for schools, later broadcast on 22 March. |
| 1968 | Conor died at his home during the evening of 5 February. |
| 1968 | Small Memorial Exhibition included in the RHA Annual Exhibition, Dublin. |
| 1968 | The RUA Annual Exhibition included a small memorial show of his work. |
| 1968 | A Retrospective Exhibition, organised by the Arts Council of Northern Ireland and entitled 'William Conor 1881–1968', was opened on 29 October, at the Ulster Museum, Belfast. |
| 1969 | Another exhibition, entitled 'William Conor 1881–1968', was held in Belfast by William Rodman & Co Ltd, and included L. A. Kaitcer (Antiques) Ltd. |
| 1969 | Queen's University Art Gallery held an exhibition of Conor's work. |
| 1969 | Exhibition of Conor's work entitled 'Children of Ulster' held at the McClelland Galleries, Belfast. |
| 1971 | Exhibition of Conor's war work entitled 'Belfast Blitz Thirty Years Ago', was held at the McClelland Galleries, Belfast. |
| 1973 | Three works included in Autumn Exhibition of Irish Artists held by William Rodman & Co, Ltd (26 Sept to 13 Oct). |
| 1974 | The Ulster Museum held an exhibition of some of Conor's work from their Permanent Collection. |
| 1975/76 | One Conor work included by the Crawford Municipal Art Gallery, Cork, in an 'Exhibition of Irish Art 1900–1950', held in association with Rosc Teoranta, which opened on 1 December, for two months. Included was Conor's *Ferryboats, River Lagan*, lent by the Ulster Museum, Belfast. |
| 1977 | Conor's *Ferryboats, River Lagan* and *City Hall Under Snow* included in 'Landscapes of Belfast', an exhibition in the Ulster Museum in association with Belfast City Festival. |
| 1978 | The Orchard Gallery, Londonderry, held an Exhibition entitled 'Portraits of Writers' (10–13 October). Included were the Conor portraits of St John Ervine, Thomas Carnduff and Richard Rowley, all lent by the Ulster Museum. |
| 1979 | An Exhibition of Paintings and Drawings from a Private Collection by William Conor and Dan O'Neill was held at Oakland Antiques, Belfast (22–29 November). |

<table>
<tr><td>1980</td><td>The Arts Council of Northern Ireland, in association with the Sports Council, held an exhibition entitled 'Sportsview' at the Arts Council Gallery, Belfast from 11 September–4 October before touring the Province. Included were two Conors on loan from the Ulster Folk and Transport Museum. No. 7, *Farmers' Race*, and No. 8, *Hurley Players*.</td></tr>
<tr><td>1980</td><td>Malone Gallery Ltd held an 'Exhibition and Sale of Paintings, Watercolours, and Drawings, by Past Irish Artists (1900–1974)' from 12 September to 11 October: included were 11 drawings and one oil painting by Conor.</td></tr>
</table>

'The end of an era'
by Rowel Friers
(*Belfast Telegraph*, 10
February 1968)

# BIBLIOGRAPHY

## Books

Books marked thus * include illustrations of Conor's work.

*Annesley, Mabel M., *As the Sight is Bent: an unfinished autobiography* ed. Constance Malleson (London: Museum Press, 1964).

**Arts in Ulster, The*, ed. Sam Hanna Bell, Nesca A. Robb, John Hewitt, (London: Harrap, 1951) (Chapter on Painting and Sculpture in Ulster by John Hewitt).

*Belfast Street Directories* 1880–1969.

*Bodkin, Thomas, *Twelve Irish Artists* (Dublin: Victor Waddington Publications, 1940).

Bourgeois, Maurice, *John Millington Synge and the Irish Theatre* (London: Constable, 1913).

Bowker, R. R., ed. *American Library Directory* (New York & London: R. R. Bowker & Co, 28th edition, 1972).

Campbell, Joseph, *Earth of Cualann* (Dublin & London: Maunsel, 1917).

Carnduff, Thomas, *Songs from the Shipyards and other Poems* (Belfast: Thornton, 1924).

Catto, Mike, *Art in Ulster 2* (Belfast: Blackstaff Press, 1977).

*Conor, William, *The Irish Scene* (Belfast: MacCord, 1944). (Foreword E. M. O'R. Dickey, Critical Appreciation by Richard Rowley).

Cooper, Douglas, *The Cubist Epoch* (London: Phaidon Press in association with the Los Angeles County Museum of Art, California, and The Metropolitan Museum of Art, New York, 1971).

Doyle, Lynn, *Ballygullion* (Dublin: Maunsel, 1908).

*——— Illustrations by William Conor, *Ballygullion* (Dublin and London: Maunsel, 1918).

——— The *Spirit of Ireland* (London: Batsford, 1935).

*——— *Ballygullion Ballads and other Verses* (London: Duckworth, 1936).

*——— *The Shake of the Bag Stories* (London: Duckworth, 1939).

*——— *A Bowl of Broth* (London: Duckworth, 1945).

*——— *Green Oranges* (London: Duckworth, 1947).

*——— *The Ballgullion Bus* (London: Duckworth, 1957).

Duveen, Sir Joseph, *Thirty Years of British Art* (London: Studio Special Autumn Number, 1930).

*Hamilton, Paul, *Up The Shankill* (Belfast: Blackstaff Press, 1979).

Hayward, Richard, *In Praise of Ulster* (Belfast: Wm. Mullan, 5th edition revised, 1946).

———*In the Kingdom of Kerry* (Dundalk: W. Tempest, Dundalgan Press, 1946).

*Hewitt, John, *Art in Ulster 1*, Bibliography by Theo Snoddy (Belfast: Blackstaff Press, 1977).

Hollins, Alfred, *A Blind Musician Looks Back: An Autobiography* (Edinburgh: Blackwood, 1936).

Hudson, Kenneth and Ann Niechoels, eds., *Directory of Museums* (London: Macmillan, 1975).

*Irvine, John, *By Winding Roads* (Belfast: H. R. Carter Publications, 1950).

Lavery, Sir John, *Life of a Painter* (London: Cassell, 1940).

MacNamara, Brinsley, *The Valley of the Squinting Windows* (London: Sampson Low, Marston, 1928).

McDowell, Florence Mary, *Roses and Rainbows* (Belfast: Blackstaff Press, 1972).

Ó Crohan, Thomás, *The Island Man*, translated from the Irish by Robin Flower

(Oxford: Clarendon Press, 1971).

Price, Victor, ed., *Apollo in Mourne: Poems Plays and Stories by Richard Rowley* (Belfast: Blackstaff Press, 1978).

Rodgers, W. R., *Irish Literary Portraits: Conversations with those who knew him* (London: British Broadcasting Corporation Publication, 1972).

*Rowley, Richard, *Pageant celebrating the Fifteen Hundredth Anniversary of the Landing of the St. Patrick at Saul, C. Down* (Belfast: 1932).

———— The Piper of Mourne and other Poems (Belfast: Derrick MacCord, 1944).

* ———— 'The Douai Version' in *The Northern Harvest: An Anthology of Ulster Writing*, ed. Robert Greacen (Belfast: Derrick MacCord, 1944).

* ———— 'The Douai Version' in *Brave Crack: an Anthology of Ulster Wit and Humour* (Belfast: H. R. Carter Publications, 1950).

Sayers, Peig, *An Old Woman's Reflections*, translated from the Irish by Séamus Ennis, introduction by W. R. Rodgers (London: Oxford University Press, 1962).

Shaw-Sparrow, Walter, *John Lavery and his Work* (Kegan Paul, Trench, Trubner).

*Shearman, Hugh, *Northern Ireland 1921–1971* (Her Majesty's Stationery Office, 1971).

*Sheringham, George, and R. Boyd Morrison, eds. for Rupert Mason, *Robes of Thespis: Costume Designs by Modern Artists* (London: Ernest Benn, 1928) (Section III. Irish Dramatic Costume).

* *The Tree 1836–1936* a centenary book (Belfast: Society for the Prevention of Cruelty to Animals, 1936).

* *An Ulster Garland 1928*, an Occasional Publication in aid of the Hospital for Sick Children Belfast (Belfast: McCaw, Stevenson & Orr, 1928).

*Walker, J. Crampton, *Irish Life and Landscape* (Dublin & Cork: Talbot Press, 1926).

*Who was Who* (London: A. & C. Black, 1951–60).

## Articles and Reviews.

Articles marked thus * include photograph of Conor or his work.

Anon, 'Portrait Drawing of Ulster Leaders', *Northern Whig and Belfast Post*, 20 December 1916.

———— 'Belfast Art Society Exhibition', *Belfast Telegraph*, 10 October 1917.

———— 'Royal Hibernian Academy Annual Exhibition', *Northern Whig and Belfast Post*, 2 April 1919.

———— 'Dawson Gallery. Specimens of an artist's work. (Dublin).' *Freemans Journal*, 26 May 1921.

* ———— 'Salon de la Nationale: William Conor', *La Revue Moderne*, 30 October 1921.

* ———— 'Mr W. Conor's Success', *Belfast Telegraph*, 23 December 1921.

———— 'Une exposition d'art irlandais', (Barbazanges Galleries, Paris), *Le Temps*, 25 February 1922.

———— 'Studio-Talk', (Goupil Gallery Exhibition, London), *The Studio*, December 1922 p. 340 & 341.

———— 'Mr William Conor's Exhibition of Pictures', (Belfast), *Northern Whig and Belfast Post*, 23 October 1923.

* ———— (Illustrations are *The Launch, Queen's Island* and *The Darlins*, two paintings exhibited at Magee Gallery, Belfast), *Irish Telegraph*, 25 October 1923.

———— 'A Belfast Artist: Remarkable Exhibition by Mr William Conor', (Belfast), *Irish Times*, 24 October 1923.

*——— 'The Art of William Conor', *Colour Magazine*, Nov/Dec 1923, Vol. 19, No. 4–5, pp. 10–12.

——— 'The Royal Academy', *Colour Magazine*, April/May 1924, Vol. 20, No. 3–4, p. 23.

*——— 'Industrial Life: William Conor's Pictures', *People's Year Book*, 1924.

——— 'Exhibition of Pictures', (Dublin). *Irish Independent*, 27 May 1925.

*——— 'Mr William Conor's Ulster Poster', *Belfast Telegraph*, 25 January 1926.

*——— 'Belfast Rotarians and Guests', *Belfast News Letter*, 27 January 1926.

*——— 'American Girls Stun Irish Artist', *Philadelphia Ledger*, 21 June 1926.

*——— (Illustration of Conor's 'At The Door'), *New York Herald Tribune*, 10 October 1926.

——— (A review of Irish Life, Babcock Galleries, New York), *Sonntagsblatt der New Yorker Volkszeitung*, 10 October 1926.

——— 'A Famous Irish Artist', *Northern Whig and Belfast Post*, 26 March 1927.

———(Review of Conor exhibition at his Belfast studio), *Irish News*, 23 May 1927.

*——— (Cover of Empire Week Programme designed by Conor), *Belfast British Empire Week*, Official Programme, 23 May 1927.

——— 'Ulster's Own Artist', *Belfast Telegraph*, 24 May 1927.

*——— 'Ulster Art and Artists. Belfast Art Society's 46th Exhibition', *Ulster Life and Opinion*, 13 October 1927, Vol. 1, No. 13, pp. 10 and 23.

——— 'Belfast British Artists' Exhibition', *Ulster Life and Opinion*, December 1927, Vol. 1, No. 15, p. 7.

*——— 'A Great Figure in Irish Presbyterianism', (Obituary of Rev. James Brown Armour), *Northern Whig and Belfast Post*, 26 January 1928.

——— 'Art Exhibitions', (Godfrey Phillips Gallery, London), *The Times*, 8 April 1929.

——— 'Godfrey Phillips Galleries', *Belfast Telegraph*, 10 April 1929.

——— 'Prominent Belfast Artist', *Belfast News Letter*, 16 April 1930.

——— 'Belfast Art Society Press Preview', *Northern Whig and Belfast Post*, 18 October 1930.

*——— (Photographs of the Belfast Art Society Exhibition.) *Belfast News Letter*, 23 October 1930.

*——— 'St. Patrick's Pageant at Castleward', *Belfast News Letter*, 6 June 1932.

——— 'Ulster Academy of Arts', *Northern Whig and Belfast Post*, 19 October 1932.

*———(Illustration of the only photograph taken of the Opening of the First Northern Ireland Parliament in 1921), *Jubilee Pictorial Souvenir*, Supplement to the *Belfast News Letter*, 4 May 1935, p. 24.

*——— 'The Richard Campbell Memorial', *The Recorder*, (Bulletin of the American Irish Historical Society) Vol. 9, No. 2, 1 June 1936, p. 4.

——— 'Our London Letter: Ulster Artist's Commission', *Northern Whig and Belfast Post*, 17 July 1936.

*——— 'His Majesty King George VI', (Conor Portrait), *Northern Whig and Belfast Post*, 24 November 1937.

*——— 'This Year's Royal Hibernian Academy', *Irish Times*, 23 March 1940.

——— 'Total Moneys Raised', *Belfast Telegraph*, 10 October 1940.

*——— 'Ulster War Effort Illustrated', (Exhibition Brands, Belfast), *Belfast Telegraph*, 3 December 1940.

——— 'Air Raid Memories', *Belfast Telegraph*, 6 August 1941.

——— 'Ulster Academy of Arts', *Belfast News Letter*, 8 October 1941.

——— 'More Pictures of U.S. Troops', *Belfast Weekly Telegraph*, 30 January 1942.

*——— 'First Soldier Reads First Issue', *Stars and Stripes*, 9 May 1942.

———— 'Ulster Arts Exhibition', *Northern Whig and Belfast Post*, 13 October 1943.

*———— 'Racing Pictures by Conor', (Waddington Gallery, Dublin), *Irish Field*, Vol. XCIV, No. 3890, 23 December 1944.

———— 'Academy of Arts', *Belfast News Letter*, 17 October 1945.

———— 'Ulster Academy of Arts', *Belfast Telegraph*, 16 October 1946.

———— 'Ulster Academy's Exhilarating Art Exhibition', *Northern Whig and Belfast Post*, 18 October 1946.

———— 'Ulster Academy of Arts; Features of the Exhibition', *Belfast News Letter*, 15 October 1947.

———— 'Ulster Art Exhibition', *Northern Whig and Belfast Post*, 15 October 1947.

———— 'London Letter: Artist's Memento', *Belfast News Letter*, 5 May 1951.

*———— 'At the R.H.A. Exhibition in Dublin', *Belfast Telegraph*, 30 April 1957.

*———— 'Portrait Gallery: William Conor', *Irish Times*, 9 October 1958.

———— 'Tribute to William Conor', *News Letter*, 9 May 1964.

———— 'Belfast of Yesterday', *Belfast Telegraph*, 24 February 1966.

*———— 'William Conor: his true stature has yet to be Assessed', *Sunday Press*, 10 February 1968.

———— 'Tributes to the late Mr William Conor', *Irish Weekly*, 17 February 1968.

———— 'Conor leaves work to "Country he loved"', *Sunday News*, 29 December 1968.

'W.A.' 'A Belfast Artist William Conor's Studio', *Northern Whig and Belfast Post*, 4 October 1924.

Alexandre, Arsène, 'La vie Artistique: L'Ecole irlandaise à Paris', *Figaro*, 27 January 1922.

Allen, Frederick, 'Ulster Academy Exhibition Opened. Ten outstanding works, 20 worthy Exhibits', *News Letter*, 16 October 1958.

L.C. (Leah Clarke), 'These are pictures of the People', *Irish Press*, 30 April 1940.

*Conor, William, (Four Conor illustrations: chalk drawings of Mill workers and of a young child, *Quittin' Time* and *Mill-girl*), *Colour Magazine*, December 1921, Vol. 15, No. 5, pp. 99, 105, 110, 112.

*———— (Conor illustration *A Shipworker*), *Colour Magazine*, January 1922, Vol. 15, No. 6, p. 139.

*———— (Conor Illustration *Half-Timer*), *Colour Magazine*, April 1922 Vol. 16, No. 3, p. 68.

*———— (Two Conor Illustrations: *A Young Belfast Mill-Girl* and *Sthrollin' Home*), Colour Magazine, May 1922, Vol. 16, No. 4, pp. 78 and 80.

*———— (Two Conor Illustrations: a woodcut and *At the Pump*) *Colour Magazine*, February 1923, Vol. 18, No. 1, pp. 18 and 26.

*———— (Conor Illustration: *Belfast Weavers*), *Colour Magazine*, August 1923, Vol. 19, No. 1, p. 20.

*———— (Conor Illustration: *Seated Girl*), *Colour Magazine*, February 1924, Vol. 20, No. 1, p. 5.

*———— (Conor cover illustration: a chalk drawing), *Colour Magazine*, March 1924, Vol. 20, No. 2.

*———— (Conor Illustration *The Studio Dance* exhibited at The Royal Academy) *Colour Magazine*, June/July 1924, Vol. 20, No. 5–6, p. 3.

———— 'My American Impressions' *Ulster Life and Opinion*, 26 May 1927, Vol. 1, No. 3, p. 13.

*———— 'An impression from memory of the Service in St. Patrick's Cathedral' (full page illustration), *Irish Times*, 5 June 1928.

*———— (Illustration of *The Gombeen Man*, British Artist's Exhibition, Liverpool), *Belfast Telegraph*, 2 March 1929.

*———— 'Where Working Girl Beats Society Beauty', *Daily Chronicle*, 30 April 1929.

*———— (Conor illustration of a chalk drawing), *Colour Magazine*, June 1930, p. 28.

*———— (Conor illustration of *Kitty* exhibiting at The Royal Portrait Society, *Colour Magazine*, December 1930, Vol. III, No. 2, p. 1.

*———— 'Barbaric Designs. Vivid Costume Scheme', *Belfast Telegraph*, 12 April 1932.

———— 'Twelfth Paintings', *Belfast Telegraph*, 10 July 1933.

———— 'An Artist's Warning', *Belfast Telegraph*, 15 March 1935.

———— 'William Conor discusses his Art', *Belfast Telegraph*, 13 July 1957.

**Daily Express* Special Representative, 'Ulster Artist's Striking Painting of Primate' (Dr. d'Arcy), *Daily Express*, 15 June 1935.

Digidon, Gerard M., 'Joseph Campbell: Recollections'. *Irish Writing*, Jan. 1950, Vol. 10, pp. 66–70.

*Doyle, Lynn, 'Empire Week in Ballygullion', (Portrait of Lynn Doyle by Conor), *Ulster Life and Opinion*, 26 May 1927, Vol. 1, No. 3, p. 7.

*Edwards, Mrs Hubert (ed.), (Cover Illustration of Conor's *Red Haired Kitty*) *G.F.S. Magazine*, October 1932.

Ervine, St. John, 'A Belfast Artist: The First Duty of a Portrait Painter', *Belfast Telegraph*, 23 February 1945.

*Furst, Herbert, 'Art News and Notes: Mr. William Conor's Crayon Drawings and Mr. Maurice Minkowski's Paintings at Mr. Godfrey Phillips Galleries, *Apollo Magazine*, April 1929, pp. 319–320.

*G.H.G., 'R.H.A. Exhibition: 1 – Oils', *Irish Times*, 25 April 1951.

*Hayward, H. Richard, 'William Conor', *Ulster Review*, October 1924, Vol. 1, No. 5, pp. 112–114.

*———— 'The Belfast Art Society', Ulster Review, November 1924' Vol. 1, No. 6, pp. 134, 136 and 141.

J.H.H. (John Hewitt), 'An Ulster Painter. The Irish Scene: Wm Conor (MacCord, Belfast)', *The Lagan*, Vol. 3, 1945.

*Jackson, Holbrook, 'Belfast', *The Studio*, October 1925, Vol. XC, No. 391, p. 260.

*Loudan, Jack, 'Famous Irishwomen' *Daily Express*, daily series beginning 15 October 1934.

*————'Conor the Sincere', *Belfast Telegraph*, 6 February 1968.

*Loudan, William Jackson, 'Mainly About Northern Folk', *Model Housekeeping*, June 1932, pp. 527 and 584.

*McCabe, Gladys, 'Art & Entertainment: Art', *Ulster Illustrated*, Summer No. 1957, Vol. 5, No. 2, pp. 12 and 13.

*McIlwaine, Eddie 'The Strain at the Top', *Ireland's Saturday Night*, 11 August 1962.

Marriott, Charles, 'Current Art. The Goupil Gallery Exhibitions', *Westminster Gazette*, 28 May 1923.

Meurville, Louis de, 'A Travers Les Expositions: L'Art en Irlande', *Gaulois*, 24 February 1923.

Millin, S. Shannon, 'William Conor The Artist', *Irish Independent*, 29 July 1924.

Mills, F. A. C., 'Ulster Artists At Pollock's Gallery (Belfast)', *Ulster Review*, August 1924, Vol. 1, No. 3, pp. 58 and 61.

*Northern Whig* Woman Correspondent, 'The Lure of Speed: Then and Now. The Impressions of an Artist', Supplement to the *Northern Whig and Belfast Post*, 20 August 1932.

W.B.R., 'An Ulster Art Exhibition' *The Bulletin*, July 1923, Vol. 1, No. 5, p. 15.

*Reeve, Alan, 'Drawing The Crowd: 7. Caricature by Alan Reeve of William Conor, A.R.H.A., R.O.I.', *Irish Times*, 6 January 1940.

Sisson, Chierbault, 'Salon de la National', *Le Temps*, Paris, 21 April 1922.

South, John, 'Celebrities in Shirt-Sleeves, Augustus John', *Everybody's Weekly*, 14 May 1927.

*Van Hoek, Kees, 'Vignette: William Conor' (caricature of Conor by Rowel Friers), *Irish Times*, 26 August 1950.

Waring, J. K., 'Belfast Cartoonist in Australia', *Ireland's Saturday Night*, 5 January 1924.

*White, James, 'Pictures for the Home', *Irish Art*, A Volume of articles and illustrations, Dublin, MCMXLIV.

Williams, R. Stephen, 'I met in Ulster: The Artist Searching for Types', *Daily Express*, 15 November 1930.

*Williams, Stephen, 'Beauty in Ulster', (illustrations by Conor), *Daily Express*, series of 6 weekly articles beginning 3 December 1930.

## Catalogues

1910–1929, 1931, 1933–1940, 1942, 1944, 1948–1968   Royal Ulster Academy Annual Exhibitions.

1916   Crayon Portrait Drawings (from life) of Sir Edward Carson, Officers and types of the Ulster Division, auctioned at The Mart, Belfast.

1918–1968   Royal Hibernian Academy Annual Exhibitions.

1921, 1924, 1928, 1930, 1932–5   Royal Society of Portrait Painters Annual Exhibitions.

1921, 1922, 1925, 1928, 1930–37, 1943   Royal Glasgow Institute of the Fine Arts Annual Exhibitions.

1921   Exhibition of Paintings and Drawings at the Dawson Gallery, Dublin.

1922   'Colour Magazine' Exhibition of Modern Art at the Grosvenor Galleries, London.

1922   Annual Summer Exhibition at the Grosvenor Galleries, London.

1922   Annual Winter Exhibition at the Grosvenor Galleries, London.

1922–24   The Goupil Gallery Salon Annual Exhibitions, London.

1925   Paintings and Drawings by William Conor, St Stephen's Green Gallery, Dublin.

1927   Exhibition of Irish Life, Babcock Galleries, New York.

1927   Loan Exhibition of Irish Portraits by Ulster Artists, Municipal Museum and Art Gallery, Belfast.

1927   Exhibition of the work of Living British Artists under the auspices of the British Artists' Exhibition, Walker Art Gallery, Liverpool.

1928   Exhibition of the work of Living British Artists under the auspices of the British Artists' Exhibition, Municipal Museum and Art Gallery, Plymouth.

1929   Exhibition of the work of Living British Artists under the auspices of the British Artists' Exhibition, Municipal Museum and Art Gallery, Belfast.

1932–37   Royal Institute of Oil Painters Annual Exhibitions, London.

1939   The Art of 79 Countries (The International Business Machines Corporation) at the New York World's Fair.

1941   Exhibition of Pictures by Conor, Robinson & Cleavers Ltd, Belfast.

1945   Royal Academy of Arts, Exhibition of National War Pictures, London.

1945–46   Exhibition of Recent Paintings by William Conor, CEMA; opened in Belfast and then toured the Province.

1950   Exhibition of Recent Pictures and Drawings by Conor (Introduction is a sonnet by John Hewitt), CEMA, Belfast.

1951   Contemporary Ulster Art, CEMA, Municipal Museum and Art Gallery, Belfast.

1951    Contemporary Ulster Paintings, Scottish Arts Council/Lewinter Frankl Collection, Edinburgh.

1951    Bangor Civic Week, Exhibition of Paintings Loaned by Bangor Residents in the Guild Hall, Bangor, Co Down, N. Ireland.

1957    William Conor Retrospective Exhibition (Introduction by John Hewitt), CEMA, Museum and Art Gallery, Belfast.

1962    Exhibition by Various Artists, CEMA in association with Dungannon Urban and Rural District Council held in the Royal School, Dungannon.

1963    Ulster Arts Club Exhibition, Ulster Museum, Belfast.

1964    William Conor, OBE, MA, RHA, Paintings and Drawings, the Bell Gallery, Belfast.

1965    Memorial Exhibition for Sam Thompson, the Bell Gallery, Belfast.

1965    Exhibition of Great Irishmen, Ulster Museum, Belfast.

1966    MacGeough Bond Collection, Ulster Museum, Belfast.

1966    Belfast of Yesterday (Foreword by Kenneth Jamison), the Bell Gallery, Belfast.

1967    Conor, the Bell Gallery, Belfast.

1968    Conor 1881–1968, Memorial Exhibition, Arts Council of Northern Ireland, Belfast.

1969    Conor 1881–1968, William Rodman & Co, Ltd, including L. A. Kaitcer (Antiques) Ltd, Belfast.

1969    William Conor, Queen's University Art Gallery, Belfast.

1969    Children of Ulster, McClelland Galleries, Belfast.

1971    The Belfast Blitz of 30 Years Ago, McClelland Galleries, Belfast.

1973    Autumn Exhibition of Irish Art, William Rodman & Co, Ltd, including L. A. Kaitcer (Antiques) Ltd, Belfast.

1974    Ulster Museum Exhibition of some of Conor's work from their Permanent Collection.

1974–75    Drawings by Conor, Carr, Blackshaw, Friers, Luke, Middleton, in an Arts Council of Northern Ireland Touring Exhibition.

1975–76    Exhibition of Irish Art 1900–1950, in association with Rosc Teoranta, the Crawford Municipal Art Gallery, Cork.

1977    Landscapes of Belfast at the Ulster Museum in association with Belfast City Festival.

1978    Portraits of Writers, Orchard Gallery, Londonderry.

1980    Sportsview, Arts Council of Northern Ireland in association with the Sports Council, Touring Exhibition.

1980    Exhibition and Sale of Paintings, Watercolours, and Drawings, by Past Irish Artists (1900–1974), Malone Gallery Ltd, Belfast.

# WORKS BY CONOR IN THE PERMANENT COLLECTIONS OF ART GALLERIES AND MUSEUMS

All dates are approximate unless marked otherwise:

| | | | |
|---|---|---|---|
| * | dated by the artist | n.d. | no date |
| beq. | bequest | pres. | presented |
| don. | donated | pur. | purchased |

| Title | Media | Size (in cm.) | Date |
|---|---|---|---|

**ENGLAND**

*THE CITY ART GALLERY MANCHESTER*

| | | | | | |
|---|---|---|---|---|---|
| 1. *Maternal Love* | pencil and crayon on paper | 36.8 × 31.7 | pur. | 1923 |
| 2. *Cronies* | ,, | 40.6 × 27.9 | pur. | 1923 |
| 3. *The Bridal Morning* (all studies for paintings) | ,, | 54 × 44.4 | pur. | 1923 |

*THE WHITWORTH ART GALLERY MANCHESTER*

| | | | | |
|---|---|---|---|---|
| 1. *The Green Shawl* | coloured chalk | 31.7 × 24.1 | pur. | 1923 |

**NORTHERN IRELAND**

*ARMAGH COUNTY MUSEUM*

| | | | |
|---|---|---|---|
| 1. *T. G. F. Paterson Esq., O.B.E., M.A., M.R.I.A.* | oil | 74.9 × 62.2 | 1953* |
| 2. *Thomas A. Montgomery Esq., D.L., J.P.* | ,, | 88.9 × 69.9 | n.d. |
| 3. *Wayside Chat* | crayon on paper | 49.5 × 49.5 | n.d. |
| 4. *Belfast Children* | lithograph | 30.5 × 24.1 | 1918* |

*THE ARTS COUNCIL OF NORTHERN IRELAND*

| | | | |
|---|---|---|---|
| 1. *College Hill, Armagh* | oil | 45.7 × 33 | n.d. |
| 2. *Hobby Horses* | ,, | 76.2 × 61 | n.d. |
| 3. *Washing Day* | ,, | 50.8 × 61 | n.d. |
| 4. *Ballad Singers* | watercolour | 30.5 × 30.5 | n.d. |
| 5. *Fares Please* | ,, | 35.6 × 35.6 | n.d. |
| 6. *Chair-o-Planes* | ,, | 35.6 × 50.8 | n.d. |

*ULSTER FOLK AND TRANSPORT MUSEUM*

| | | | |
|---|---|---|---|
| 1. *Picture House Queue* (Shankill Rd., Belfast) | oil on canvas | 91.4 × 71.1 | 1930–34 |
| 2. *Men of Iron* (Study for 'The Launch', Belfast Shipyard) | ,, ,, ,, | 106.7 × 48.3 | 1922 |
| 3. *Hillsborough Hunt* (Hillsborough, Co Down) | ,, ,, ,, | 61 × 50.8 | 1950 |
| 4. *Delph Woman* (Belfast) | ,, ,, ,, | 50.8 × 40.6 | 1912 |
| 5. *The Potato Diggers* (Dromara, Co Down) | ,, ,, ,, | 50.8 × 40.6 | 1948 |

| | | | |
|---|---|---|---|
| 6. *Women of the Field* (Co Antrim) | Oil on canvas | 50.8 × 40.6 | 1948 |
| 7. *Trees on the Lagan* (near Shaw's Bridge) | ,, ,, ,, | 50.8 × 40.6 | 1935 |
| 8. *The Politician* | ,, ,, ,, | 45.7 × 35.6 | 1925 |
| 9. *The Twelfth* (Wellington Place, Belfast) | ,, ,, ,, | 91.4 × 71.1 | 1918 |
| 10. *Testing his Steps* | ,, ,, ,, | 50.8 × 40.6 | 1920 |
| 11. *The Jaunting Car* (at end of Orange Procession | ,, ,, ,, | 50.8 × 61 | 1933 |
| 12. *Carrying Potatoes* (near Ballyclare, Co Antrim) | ,, ,, ,, | 50.8 × 61 | 1939 |
| 13. *The Reader* | ,, ,, ,, | 45.7 × 61 | 1939 |
| 14. *Gathering Seaweed* (Co Donegal) | ,, ,, ,, | 50.8 × 40.6 | 1935 |
| 15. *Open Air Market* (Co Antrim) | ,, ,, ,, | 50.8 × 50.8 | 1930 |
| 16. *The Concertina Player* (Ballyclare, Co Antrim) | ,, ,, ,, | 76.2 × 63.5 | 1930 |
| 17. *Fun of the Fair* (Lammas Fair, Ballycastle, Co Antrim) | ,, ,, ,, | 76.2 × 63.5 | 1935 |
| 18. *Music in the Park* (Botanic Gardens, Belfast) | ,, ,, ,, | 76.2 × 63.5 | 1947 |
| 19. *Strangford* (Looking towards Portaferry, Co Down) | ,, ,, ,, | 76.2 × 63.5 | 1934 |
| 20. *The Block-wheel Cart* (Co Antrim) | ,, ,, ,, | 91.4 × 71.1 | 1920 |
| 21. *Going to the Mills* (Crumlin Rd., Belfast) | lead pencil on paper | 127 × 101.6 | 1914 |
| 22. *Weavers* | ,, ,, ,, ,, | 39 × 56 | n.d. |
| 23. *Eleventh Night* (Shankhill Rd., Belfast) | crayon on paper | 38.1 × 30.5 | 1912 |
| 24. *Close off Durham Street* (Belfast) | ,, ,, ,, | 43.2 × 30.5 | 1907 |
| 25. *Belfast Mill Girl* | ,, ,, ,, | 30.5 × 25.4 | 1907 |
| 26. *Potato Harvest* (Portadown, Co Armagh) | ,, ,, ,, | 27.9 × 22.9 | 1910 |
| 27. *The Passing Stranger* (Old Lodge Rd., Belfast) | ,, ,, ,, | 35.6 × 27.9 | 1908 |
| 28. *Gathering Potatoes* (near Strangford, Co Down) | ,, ,, ,, | 40.6 × 48.3 | 1945 |
| 29. *Ardglass Fisher Girls* (Co Down) | ,, ,, ,, | 50.8 × 40.6 | 1945 |
| 30. *Homewards* (West Co Donegal) | ,, ,, ,, | 40.6 × 30.9 | 1925 |
| 31. *Lamp Post Swinging* (Belfast) | ,, ,, ,, | 50.8 × 40.6 | 1957 |
| 32. *Mother and Child* (Crumlin, Co Antrim) | ,, ,, ,, | 50.8 × 40.6 | 1909 |
| 33. *To the Mainland* (off Co Kerry) | ,, ,, ,, | 50.8 × 40.6 | 1939 |
| 34. *Potato Digging* (Crumlin, Co Antrim) | ,, ,, ,, | 50.8 × 40.6 | 1910 |
| 35. *The Hobby Horses* (Belfast) | ,, ,, ,, | 50.8 × 40.6 | 1951 |
| 36. *Sunday Morning* (Belfast) | ,, ,, ,, | 35.6 × 27.9 | 1911 |
| 37. *Gossiping* (Old Lodge Rd., Belfast) | ,, ,, ,, | 35.6 × 27.9 | 1910 |
| 38. *At the Pump* (Greencastle, Co Antrim) | ,, ,, ,, | 50.8 × 40.6 | 1932 |
| 39. *The Farmers' Race* (Lisnalinchy, Co Down) | ,, ,, ,, | 61 × 50.8 | 1932 |
| 40. *The Hurley Players* (Falls Park, Belfast) | ,, ,, ,, | 61 × 50.8 | 1948 |
| 41. *The Flute Band* (Limavady, Co Londonderry) | ,, ,, ,, | 61 × 50.8 | 1950 |
| 42. *Within the Lights of Belfast* | ,, ,, ,, | 22.9 × 17.8 | 1908 |
| 43. *Self Portrait* | ,, ,, ,, | 58.4 × 45.7 | n.d. |
| 44. *Three Generations* | ,, ,, ,, | 68.6 × 45.7 | 1918 |
| 45. *Saturday Morning* (Belfast) | pen and ink and crayon on paper | 33 × 22.9 | 1906* |
| 46. *Cronies* | pen and ink and crayon on paper | 20.3 × 14 | 1907* |
| 47. *The Jaunting Car* (Belfast) | pen and ink and crayon on paper | 22.9 × 30.5 | 1931 |

| | | | | |
|---|---|---|---|---|
| 48. | *A Bit of a 'Crack'* (Belfast) | pen and ink and crayon on paper | 22.9 × 27.9 | 1909 |
| 49. | *York Street* (Belfast) | pen and ink and crayon on paper | 22.9 × 17.8 | 1908 |
| 50. | *A Group of Mill Girls* (Belfast) | pen and ink on paper | 25.4 × 20.3 | 1906* |
| 51. | *At the Empire* (Empire Theatre, Belfast) | ,, ,, ,, ,, ,, | 22.9 × 17.8 | 1910* |
| 52. | *Cronies* (Belfast) | ,, ,, ,, ,, ,, | 22.9 × 17.8 | 1909* |
| 53. | *Out for a 'Dander'* (West Co Donegal) | ,, ,, ,, ,, ,, | 22.9 × 17.8 | 1907* |
| 54. | *The Ice-Cream Cart* (York St., Belfast) | pen and ink and watercolour on paper | 22.9 × 17.8 | 1908* |
| 55. | *The Back Yard* | watercolour on paper | 27.9 × 21.6 | n.d. |
| 56. | *Armagh* | woodcut on paper | 34 × 27 | n.d. |

*THE ULSTER MUSEUM*

| | | | | |
|---|---|---|---|---|
| 1. | *City Hall under Snow* | oil on canvas on board | 42.9 × 53.3 | n.d. |
| 2. | *Courtin'* | oil on canvas | 75.6 × 50.2 | pur. 1922 |
| 3. | *Latest News 1922* | ,, ,, ,, | 48.2 × 35.5 | 1922* |
| 4. | *The Jaunting Car* | ,, ,, ,, | sight 70.5 × 90.5 | 1933 {pres. 1936 |
| 5. | *Building an Air Raid Shelter* | ,, ,, ,, | 58.4 × 47.9 | 1940 |
| 6. | *The Warden* | ,, ,, ,, | 49.8 × 39.4 | 1940 |
| 7. | *R. V. Williams* (Richard Rowley) | ,, ,, ,, | 87 × 68.6 | 1920 {don. 1935 |
| 8. | *St. John Ervine 1883–1971* | ,, ,, ,, | 76.2 × 63.5 | 1946 {don. 1965 |
| 9. | *Alderman J. A. Doran, J.P.* | ,, ,, ,, | sight 74.6 × 62.4 | 1930* |
| 10. | *The Painter's Mother* | ,, ,, ,, | sight 74 × 60.6 | 1919 {don. 1957 |
| 11. | *Self Portrait ('1825')* | ,, ,, ,, | sight 54.6 × 37.8 | 1920 {don. 1957 |
| 12. | *The Melodeon Player* | ,, ,, ,, | sight 90.2 × 69.8 | pur. 1922 |
| 13. | *Ulster Past and Present* | ,, ,, ,, | 205.7 × 749.3 | 1932* |
| 14. | *Children at the Building of a Shelter* | crayon on paper | 38.2 × 28 | 1940 |
| 15. | *Recruiting Parade* | ,, ,, ,, | 35.5 × 45.5 | 1940 |
| 16. | *Men Working at a Shelter* | ,, ,, ,, | 38 × 27.8 | 1940 |
| 17. | *A Group of Evacuees* | ,, ,, ,, | 38 × 27.8 | 1940 |
| 18. | *Study for Recruiting Parade, Bandsmen* Reverse: *Lola Montez* | ,, ,, ,, charcoal on paper | 50.6 × 37.9 | 1940 |
| 19. | *Shipyard Workers Crossing Queen's Bridge* (Study for *Men of the Home Front*) | crayon on paper | 38.2 × 27.9 | 1940 |
| 20. | *Men of the Home Front* | ,, ,, ,, | 37.8 × 54.2 | 1940 |
| 21. | *Shipyard Workers Crossing Queen's Bridge, Belfast* | ,, ,, ,, | 34.5 × 46.8 | 1940 {don. 1947 |
| 22. | *A Sergeant of the A.T.S.* | crayon on paper | 38.2 × 27.9 | 1940 |
| 23. | *Evacuees at Gt. Northern Station* | ,, ,, ,, | sight 34 × 44.5 | 1940 |
| 24. | *Evacuation of Children, Gt. Northern Railway, Belfast* | pencil and wax crayon on paper | 34.5 × 46 | 1940 {don. 1947 |
| 25. | *Soldier on Point Duty* | crayon on paper | 51.7 × 38.2 | 1940 |
| 26. | *A Piper of the Irish Fusiliers* | ,, ,, ,, | 53.3 × 36 | 1940 |
| 27. | *'Skins' on a Route March* | ,, ,, ,, | 42.7 × 34.4 | 1940 |
| 28. | *The Old Brigade* | ,, ,, ,, | 50.9 × 33.6 | 1940 |

| | | | | | |
|---|---|---|---|---|---|
| 29. | *Men of Iron* | pencil and watercolour on paper | 47.4 × 34 | | 1940 |
| 30. | *Riveting* | watercolour on paper | 45.5 × 35.5 | | 1940 |
| 31. | *Lesson on a Bren Gun* | crayon on paper | 34.2 × 44 | | 1940 |
| 32. | *Grenade Throwing Practice* | ,, ,, ,, | 45 × 34.3 | | 1940 |
| 33. | *Study for Grenade Throwing Practice* | ,, ,, ,, | 38.2 × 28.2 | | 1940 |
| 34. | *F.A.N.Y.'s Crossing Donegall Place, Belfast* | ,, ,, ,, | 47.8 × 29 | | 1940 |
| 35. | *Soldier's Wedding* | ,, ,, ,, | 46 × 37.9 | | 1940 |
| | Reverse: *Caroline Norton* | ,, ,, ,, | 37.8 × 54.2 | | |
| 36. | *Girls at Munitions* | ,, ,, ,, | 39.5 × 29 | | 1940 |
| 37. | *A Roof Spotter* | ,, ,, ,, | 45.5 × 35.4 | | 1940 |
| 38. | *Looking at Aeroplanes* | ,, ,, ,, | 50.9 × 34.6 | | 1940 |
| 39. | *Evacuee Children* | ,, ,, ,, | 38.1 × 27.7 | | 1940 |
| 40. | *Collecting Scrap Metal* | ,, ,, ,, | sight 34.7 × 44.5 | | 1940 |
| 41. | *Passing the City Hall, Belfast during a Recruiting March* | ,, ,, ,, | sight 35 × 44.5 | don. don. | 1947 1947 1941 |
| 42. | *Tramway Depot* | ,, ,, ,, | sight 44 × 33.7 | don. | 1947 |
| 43. | *Ulster Rifleman's Wedding* | ,, ,, ,, | sight 37 × 52.5 | don. | 1947 |
| 44. | *The Recruit* | pencil and watercolour on paper | sight 28 × 21 | | 1914* |
| 45. | *Fight and Endure* | pencil and watercolour on paper | 35 × 24.3 | | 1914* |
| 46. | *Off! The Ulster Division* | charcoal and red chalk on paper | 55 × 37.3 | | 1915* |
| 47. | *Bugler, Ulster Division* | charcoal and chalk on paper | 55 × 37.9 | | 1916* |
| 48. | *Two Soldiers and a Girl* | pencil and crayon on paper | 30 × 22.9 | | n.d. |
| 49. | *The Signals* | pencil and watercolour on paper | 28.4 × 39.5 | pur. | 1929 |
| 50. | *Study for the Lost Child* | crayon on paper | 86.8 × 57.8 | don. | 1922 |
| 51. | *Ferryboats, River Lagan* | pencil and watercolour on paper | 28.5 × 39.3 | pur. | 1929 |
| 52. | *Collin Glen, Belfast* | pencil and watercolour on paper | 39 × 28.5 | pur. | 1930 |
| 53. | *Thomas Carnduff (1886–1956)* | crayon on paper | 38.3 × 28 | don. | 1943 1947 |
| 54. | *The Riveter* | chalk on paper | sight 43.5 × 29.6 | | n.d. |
| 55. | *Miss Colette O'Niel (Lady Constance Malleson)* | crayon on 3-ply wood | 88.7 × 68.2 | | 24 July 1927* |
| 56. | *Leslie Montgomery* (Lynn Doyle) | crayon on paper | 41.9 × 33 | | n.d. |
| 57. | *Weavers* | coloured crayons on white paper | sight 45 × 30.1 | | n.d. |

REPUBLIC OF IRELAND

*THE HUGH LANE GALLERY, DUBLIN*

| | | | | | |
|---|---|---|---|---|---|
| 1. | *A Sup of Tea* | oil on board | 60 × 49.5 | beq. | 1961 |
| 2. | *The Mote* | watercolour | 61 × 47 | pres. | 1924 |
| 3. | *The Ould Shawl* | ,, | 28.6 × 20.3 | pres. | 1944 |
| 4. | 16 Costume Sketches of Irish Historical Figures | pastels on paper | 52.1 × 34.3 each | | 1932 |

## THE BROOKLYN MUSEUM, NEW YORK

| | | | | |
|---|---|---|---|---|
| 1. *Youth and Age* | wax crayon on paper | 63.8 × 44.4 | pur. | 1927 |
| 2. *At the Pump* | oil on canvas | 61 × 45.7 | pres. | 1926 |

# WORKS BY WILLIAM CONOR
## LISTED IN CATALOGUES
## OF MAJOR ANNUAL EXHIBITIONS.

| year | media | number | subject | price |
|---|---|---|---|---|

### The Goupil Gallery Salon, London

| year | media | number | subject | price |
|---|---|---|---|---|
| 1922 | oil | 211 | *The Dance* | £ 40. 0.0. |
| | w/c, | 255 | *The Belfast Street Singers* | £ 20. 0.0. |
| | drawings, | 344 | *The Gossips* | £ 15. 0.0. |
| | etc. | | | |
| 1923 | w/c and | 348 | *Gunman* | £ 8. 0.0. |
| | pastels | | | |
| 1924 | oil | 128 | *The Reader* | £ 21. 0.0. |
| | w/c, | | | |
| | pastels, | 349 | *The Black Shawl* | £ 8. 0.0. |
| | etc. | | | |

### The Grosvenor Galleries, London

| year | media | number | subject | price |
|---|---|---|---|---|
| 1922 (summer) | drawing | 147 | *The Street Preacher* | no prices |
| 1922 (winter) | oil | 126 | *At The Half-Door* | no prices |

### The Royal Academy of Arts, London

| year | media | number | subject | price |
|---|---|---|---|---|
| 1921 | oil | 448 | *'1820'* | |
| | | 618 | *Master H. W. R. Wallace* | |
| 1924 | ,, | 585 | *The Studio Dance* | |
| 1927 | ,, | 300 | *The Black Frock* | |
| 1931 | ,, | 444 | *Red-haired Kitty* | |
| 1932 | ,, | 52 | *The Orange Procession* | |
| 1935 | ,, | 633 | *Peddlers* | no prices |
| 1937 | ,, | 450 | *Strangford Lough, Co Down* | |
| 1938 | ,, | 467 | *Before the Curtain rises* | |
| | | 506 | *Waiting for the Excursion Train* | |
| 1939 | ,, | 298 | *The Queue* | |
| | | 374 | *R. M. Smyllie, Esq.* | |

### The Royal Glasgow Institute of the Fine Arts

| year | media | number | subject | price |
|---|---|---|---|---|
| 1921 | drawing | 665 | *Crayon drawing of a Youth's Head* | £ 50. 0.0. |
| 1922 | ,, | 615 | *In the Street* | £ 8. 8.0. |
| 1925 | w/c | 452 | *The Launch* (illustrated) | £ 26. 5.0. |
| | oil | 568 | *At the Door* | £ 26. 5.0. |
| 1928 | drawing | 788 | *The Water-carriers* | £ 12.12.0. |

| 1930 | oil | 321 | *The Jaunting Car* | £100. 0.0. |
| | ,, | 349 | *The Melodeon Player* | £ 25. 0.0. |
| | drawing | 736 | *Up the Hill* | £ 12.12.0. |
| 1931 | oil | 311 | *Patchwork Quilt* | £ 25. 0.0. |
| | ,, | 322 | *The Gospel Meeting* | £ 30. 0.0. |
| | ,, | 451 | *Saturday Night* | £ 84. 0.0. |
| 1932 | ,, | 161 | *Over the Wall* | £ 30. 0.0. |
| | | 540 | *The Unemployed* | £150. 0.0. |
| 1933 | ,, | 461 | *The Painter's Mother* | £ 78.15.0. |
| 1934 | ,, | 411 | *The Politician* | £ 15. 0.0. |
| 1935 | ,, | 199 | *The Galway Blazer* | £ 50. 0.0. |
| | ,, | 307 | *The Heater-Boy* | £ 15. 0.0. |
| | ,, | 376 | *An Ulster Market Town* | £ 75. 0.0. |
| 1936 | ,, | 134 | *Curiosity* | £ 21. 0.0. |
| | ,, | 138 | *The Water-Carrier* | £ 21. 0.0. |
| 1937 | ,, | 158 | *The Horse Parade* | £ 75. 0.0. |
| 1939 | ,, | 530 | *Before the Curtain Rises* | £ 40. 0.0. |
| | ,, | 348 | *Waiting for the Excursion Train* | £ 50. 0.0. |
| 1943 | ,, | 368 | *It's One of Ours* | £ 75. 0.0. |

## The Royal Hibernian Academy of Arts, Dublin

(Media mentioned where possible.)

| 1918 | oil | 131 | Portrait | ——— |
| | w/c, | 264 | Crayon drawing—*The Darlin* | £ 5. 5.0. |
| | drawings, | 269 | *Portrait of Major Peter Kerr Smiley,* | |
| | etc. | | *M.P.* | ——— |
| | ,, | 270 | *Crayon drawing of a Girl's Head* | £ 5. 5.0. |
| | ,, | 284 | *Balloon Man* | £ 21. 0.0. |
| | ,, | 285 | *Portrait of Lieut-Col Sir James Craig,* | |
| | | | *Bart, M.P.* | ——— |
| 1919 | oil | 137 | *Mill Workers* | £100. 0.0. |
| | ,, | 191 | *Brother and Sister* | £ 40. 0.0. |
| | w/c, etc. | 321 | *The Street-Singers* | £ 21. 0.0. |

(Note: only six other works were priced at £100 or more)

| 1920 | w/c, | 214 | *Mill Girl, Belfast* | £ 10. 0.0. |
| | etc. | 331 | *Quittin-time* | £ 6. 0.0. |
| 1921 | oil | 4 | *Miss Muriel Stewart* | ——— |
| | w/c, etc. | 277 | *Light and Shade* | £ 8. 8.0. |
| 1922 | Did not exhibit | | | |
| 1923 | Did not exhibit | | | |
| 1924 | oil | 122 | *Richard Rowley, Esq.* | ——— |
| 1925 | ,, | 13 | *At the Pump* | £ 31.10.0. |
| | ,, | 166 | *'1825'* (self-portrait) | £ 31.10.0. |
| | w/c, etc. | 270 | *Black Shawl* | £ 8. 0.0. |
| | ,, ,, | 274 | *The Reader* | £ 15.15.0. |
| | ,, ,, | 276 | *The Open Door* | £ 15.15.0. |
| 1926 | oil | 177 | *The Red-haired Boy* | ——— |
| | w/c, etc. | 254 | *The Queen's Bridge, Belfast* | £ 12.12.0. |
| | ,, ,, | 320 | *H. O. Meredith, Esq.* | ——— |
| | ,, ,, | 323 | *Resting* | £ 10.10.0. |
| 1927 | Did not exhibit | | | |

| | | | | |
|---|---|---|---|---|
| 1928 | oil | 174 | *The Accompanist* | £110. 0.0. |
| | ,, | 178 | *The Cellist* | £ 31.10.0. |
| | w/c, etc. | 230 | *The Knife-grinder* | £ 15.15.0. |
| | ,,    ,, | 238 | *At the Pump* | £ 15.15.0. |
| 1929 | Did not exhibit | | | |
| 1930 | Did not exhibit | | | |
| 1931 | Did not exhibit | | | |
| 1932 | Did not exhibit | | | |
| 1933 | oil | 40 | *The Horse Parade* | £120. 0.0. |
| | ,, | 134 | *The Jaunting Car* | £130. 0.0. |
| 1934 | Did not exhibit | | | |
| 1935 | Did not exhibit | | | |
| 1936 | oil | 61 | *'1836'* | £ 50. 0.0. |
| | ,, | 80 | *Horses and Jockeys* | £ 75. 0.0. |
| | ,, | 167 | *The Water Bearer* | £ 25. 0.0. |
| | ,, | 196 | *Miss Y* | £125. 0.0. |
| 1937 | ,, | 16 | *The Horse Fair* | £ 50. 0.0. |
| | ,, | 35 | *The Delf-Woman* | £ 30. 0.0. |
| | ,, | 111 | *R. M. Smyllie, Esq.* | ——— |
| | ,, | 118 | *Market Day* | £115. 0.0. |

Conor elected an Associate of the Academy in October 1938
(Note: only four other pictures priced higher than £220)

| | | | | |
|---|---|---|---|---|
| 1938 | oil | 178 | *The Queue* | £220. 0.0. |
| 1939 | ,, | 150 | *Market Women* | £ 27. 6.0. |
| | ,, | 176 | *Dr Douglas Hyde, President of Ireland* | ——— |
| | ,, | 181 | *Waiting for the Excursion Train* | £ 70. 0.0. |
| | ,, | 191 | *Mrs Seymour Heatly* | ——— |
| | ,, | 206 | *Strangford Lough, Co Down* | £ 70. 0.0. |
| 1940 | ,, | 8 | *J. J. Simington, Esq.* | ——— |
| | ,, | 15 | *The Winner* | £ 75. 0.0. |
| | ,, | 36 | *Rev. William Anderson M.A., Headmaster of Mountjoy School 1896–1939* | ——— |
| | w/c, etc. | 205 | *Potato Digging* | £ 12.12.0. |
| | ,,    ,, | 247 | *Master Rupert Charles* | ——— |
| | ,,    ,, | 252 | *The Jade-green Earrings* | £ 12.12.0. |
| 1941 | oil | 69 | *Mrs John Millen* | ——— |
| | ,, | 94 | *The Painter's Mother* | ——— |
| | ,, | 200 | *Exercising Greyhounds* | £ 63. 0.0. |
| | w/c, etc. | 287 | *Fisher Girls – Ardglass, Co Down* | £ 14.14.0. |
| | ,,    ,, | 294 | *The Bargeman's Wife* | £ 14.14.0. |
| | ,,    ,, | 295 | *Portrait of a Girl's Head* | ——— |
| 1942 | oil | 36 | *Before The Curtain Rises* | £ 50. 0.0. |
| | ,, | 164 | *To the Tune of the Melodeon* | ——— |
| | ,, | 168 | *The Cattle Auction* | £100. 0.0. |
| | ,, | 185 | *The Black Hat* | £130. 0.0. |
| | w/c, etc. | 266 | *The Secret* | £ 15.15.0. |
| 1943 | oil | 60 | *On the Chute* | £ 75. 0.0. |
| | ,, | 72 | *Waiting Their Turn* | £ 50. 0.0. |
| | ,, | 207 | *Fionnuala* | £ 75. 0.0. |
| | w/c, etc. | 227 | *Over the Bridge* | £ 18.18.0. |
| | ,,    ,, | 284 | *Here They Come* | £ 16.16.0. |
| | ,,    ,, | 321 | *Dr James Ashe* | ——— |
| 1944 | oil | 22 | *The Singing Class* | £ 60. 0.0. |

| | | | | |
|---|---|---|---|---|
| | oil | 113 | *Portrait of a Friend* | ———— |
| | ,, | 150 | *The Old Clothes Man* | £140. 0.0. |
| | ,, | 220 | *A Near Relation* | |
| | w/c, etc. | 229 | *Swing High Swing Low!* | £ 18.18.0. |
| | ,, ,, | 233 | *Pulling in* | £ 16.16.0. |
| 1945 | oil | 4 | *The Farmers Race* | £ 60. 0.0. |
| | ,, | 86 | *Raymond* | |
| | ,, | 186 | *It's One of Ours* | £150. 0.0. |
| | w/c, etc. | 217 | *The Mountains o' Mourne* | £ 18.18.0. |
| 1946 | oil | 2 | *The Ferry* | £ 50. 0.0. |
| | ,, | 32 | *Eve's Daughters* | £100. 0.0. |
| | w/c, etc. | 80 | *Armagh* | £ 18.18.0. |
| | oil | 158 | *Miss Gladys Woods* | ———— |

(Note: Conor elected a full member of the Academy in 1947)

| | | | | |
|---|---|---|---|---|
| 1947 | oil | 43 | *Amelia* | ———— |
| | ,, | 114 | *Hobby Horses* | £125. 0.0. |
| | ,, | 147 | *Cantering to the Starting Gate* | £ 50. 0.0. |
| | w/c, etc. | 216 | *The Widow-Woman* | £ 18. 0.0. |
| | ,, ,, | 220 | *The Tin Whistle* | £ 18. 0.0. |
| | ,, ,, | 222 | *Strangford Lough* | £ 16. 0.0. |
| 1948 | oil | 55 | *Stepping Out* | £115. 0.0. |
| | ,, | 59 | *The Musicianer* | £120. 0.0. |
| | ,, | 102 | *Young David* | £ 70. 0.0. |
| | w/c, etc. | 161 | *Gathering Potatoes* | £ 21. 0.0. |
| | ,, ,, | 173 | *The Sulky Child* | £ 20. 0.0. |
| | ,, ,, | 178 | *On the Lagan Banks* | £ 20. 0.0. |
| 1949 | oil | 15 | *Listening to the Band* | £130. 0.0. |
| | ,, | 63 | *The Path through the Woods* | £ 65. 0.0. |
| | ,, | 70 | *The Flax Gatherers* | £ 63. 0.0. |
| | ,, | 76 | *Going to the Races* | £ 55. 0.0. |
| | w/c, etc. | 189 | *On Lagan Banks* | £ 18.18.0. |
| | ,, ,, | 207 | *Churning Butter* | 21 gns. |
| 1950 | oil | 61 | *The Singing Bird* | £ 70. 0.0. |
| | ,, | 80 | *Robert Lynd* | ———— |
| | ,, | 189 | *Standing Room Only* | £ 60. 0.0. |
| | w/c, etc. | 221 | *Rest, and be thankful* | £ 21. 0.0. |
| 1951 | oil | 27 | *The Rt. Hon. Lord Farnham D.S.O.* | ———— |
| | ,, | 40 | *The Shuggleshoo* | £ 60. 0.0. |
| | ,, | 93 | *Showing his Paces* | £ 60. 0.0. |
| | w/c, etc. | 200 | *The Mouth-Organ* | £ 21. 0.0. |
| | ,, ,, | 204 | *The Chair-o-Planes* | £ 22. 0.0. |
| 1952 | oil | 15 | *The Launch* | £150. 0.0. |
| | ,, | 36 | *Altogether with the Chorus* | £150. 0.0. |
| | w/c, etc. | 226 | *Fife and Drums* | £ 26. 5.0. |
| | ,, ,, | 229 | *Mother and Child* | £ 23. 0.0. |
| 1953 | oil | 15 | *Coming from Mass* | £ 70. 0.0. |
| | ,, | 74 | *Portrait in Black and Green* | ———— |
| | ,, | 81 | *Cinema Queue* | £250. 0.0. |
| | ,, | 104 | *The Drop Stitch* | £ 60. 0.0. |
| | w/c, etc. | 183 | *When Day is Done* | £ 25. 0.0. |
| | ,, ,, | 185 | *The Wayside Cottage* | £ 21. 0.0. |
| 1954 | oil | 13 | *The Hurley Boys* | £ 70. 0.0. |
| | ,, | 112 | *Miss Blanche Bennet* | ———— |
| | w/c, etc. | 141 | *The Basket of Apples* | £ 25. 0.0. |

| | | | | |
|---|---|---|---|---|
| 1955 | oil | 43 | *The Cattle Auction* | £ 65. 0.0. |
| | ,, | 77 | *Washing Day* | £ 65. 0.0. |
| | ,, | 92 | *Fun of the Fair* | £130. 0.0. |
| | w/c, etc. | 134 | *Queue Here* | £ 25. 0.0. |
| | ,,    ,, | 137 | *The Women Next Door* | £ 23. 0.0. |
| 1956 | oil | 33 | *Fred Story, Belfast* | ———— |
| | ,, | 82 | *The Whirl of the Dance*<br>(lent by Mrs K. Smyllie) | ———— |
| | ,, | 89 | *Here Comes the Bride* | £130. 0.0. |
| | w/c, etc. | 117 | *Sean Kavanagh*<br>(lent by Prof David Greene) | ———— |
| | ,,    ,, | 134 | *Funny Mister Punch* | £ 24. 0.0. |
| | ,,    ,, | 138 | *Delgany, Co Wicklow* | £ 18. 0.0. |
| 1957 | oil | 19 | *Beero* | n.f.s. |
| | ,, | 40 | *Gathering Potatoes* | £ 63. 0.0. |
| | w/c | 50 | *Captain John W. Storey* | n.f.s. |
| | ,, | 140 | *With a Smile and a Song* | £ 31.10.0. |
| | ,, | 160 | *Going to Mass, Co Kerry* | £ 26. 5.0. |
| | ,, | 164 | *Up and Over* | £ 25. 4.0. |
| 1958 | oil | 59 | *The Whisper* | £ 57.15.0. |
| | ,, | 79 | *The March of the Strikers* | £210. 0.0. |
| | ,, | 97 | *Toilers* | £ 42. 0.0. |
| | w/c, etc. | 172 | *Horse Display* | £ 31.10.0. |
| | ,,    ,, | 176 | *Sally* | £ 27. 6.0. |
| | ,,    ,, | 186 | *Still Waters* | £ 21. 0.0. |
| 1959 | oil | 92 | *It Has Rained All Day* | £141.15.0. |
| | ,, | 107 | *A Hunting We Will Go* | ———— |
| | w/c, etc. | 127 | *Between the Dances* | £ 26. 5.0. |
| | ,,    ,, | 155 | *Off to the Starting Gate* | £ 24. 0.0. |
| | ,,    ,, | 160 | *Once on a Time* | £ 25. 4.0. |
| | ,,    ,, | 161 | *Still Waters* | £ 21. 0.0. |
| 1960 | oil | 39 | *The Slighted Child* | £105. 0.0. |
| | ,, | 92 | *The Kidney Punch* | £ 75. 0.0. |
| | ,, | 111 | *Poll Day* | £130. 0.0. |
| | w/c, etc. | 135 | *The Home Road* | £ 23. 0.0. |
| | ,,    ,, | 152 | *The Encore* | £ 21. 0.0. |
| | ,,    ,, | 159 | *Deck Chairs* | £ 25. 0.0. |
| 1961 | oil | 29 | *Over and Away* | £140. 0.0. |
| | ,, | 60 | *A Cup of Tay* | £ 50. 0.0. |
| | ,, | 96 | *The Music that Charms* | £135. 0.0. |
| | w/c, etc. | 146 | *The Variety Market* | £ 25. 0.0. |
| | ,,    ,, | 154 | *The Meet of the Co Down Stag Hounds* | £ 18. 0.0. |
| 1962 | oil | 31 | *The Happy Flute* | £140. 0.0. |
| | ,, | 146 | *The Heavy Child* | £ 52. 0.0. |
| | w/c, etc. | 169 | *Tired* | £ 50. 0.0. |
| | crayon | 177 | *A Friend o' Mine* | £ 50. 0.0. |
| | ,, | 195 | *Full House* | £ 22. 0.0. |
| | w/c | 207 | *The Drummers* | £ 24. 0.0. |
| 1963 | oil | 6 | *At the end of the Hunt* | £ 80. 0.0. |
| | ,, | 58 | *Long, Long Ago* | £120. 0.0. |
| | ,, | 109 | *An Only Child* | £ 80. 0.0. |
| | w/c, etc. | 154 | *The End of the Day* | £ 26. 0.0. |
| | ,,    ,, | 158 | *'Raise Your Voices'* | £ 30. 0.0. |
| | ,,    ,, | 219 | *The Markets* | £ 25. 0.0. |

| 1964 | oil | 42 | *All Alone Am I* | £120. 0.0. |
| | ,, | 55 | *Ne'er-Do-Well* | £110. 0.0. |
| | ,, | 150 | *Hear my Song* | £ 75. 0.0. |
| | w/c, etc. | 169 | *The Odd Child* | £ 28. 0.0. |
| | ,, ,, | 173 | *Point to Point* | £ 26. 0.0. |
| | ,, ,, | 180 | *Clothes Washing* | £ 26. 0.0. |
| 1965 | oil | 96 | *Songs of Praise* | £126. 0.0. |
| | ,, | 127 | *Hear My Song* | £ 75. 0.0. |
| | w/c, etc. | 163 | *It's High Over the Fence* | £ 26. 0.0. |
| | ,, ,, | 171 | *The Odd Child* | £ 26. 0.0. |
| 1966 | oil | 47 | *Churning Butter* | £ 42. 0.0. |
| | ,, | 71 | *Drying her Hair* | £136. 0.0. |
| | ,, | 140 | *Belfast Opera House in Days Gone By* | £147. 0.0. |
| | w/c, etc. | 167 | *Raise Your Voices* | £ 31.10.0. |
| 1967 | oil | 52 | *Come Let us be Merry* | £110. 0.0. |
| | w/c, etc. | 186 | *Fairy Footsteps* | £ 30. 0.0. |
| | ,, ,, | 201 | *Over and Away* | £ 26. 0.0. |
| | ,, ,, | 202 | *Dreamy Afternoon* | £ 25. 0.0. |

1968 Memorial Screen

| | oil | 1 | *The Whirl of the Dance* | ⎫ | Lent by |
| | ,, | 2 | *Old Woman and Child* | ⎬ | Mrs Kathleen Smyllie |
| | ,, | 3 | *The Orange Drum* | ⎭ | |
| | ,, | 4 | *A Sup of Tea* | ⎫ | Lent by |
| | ,, | 5 | *The Mote* | ⎬ | Municipal Gallery |
| | ,, | 6 | *The Ould Shaw* | ⎭ | Advisory Committee |
| | ,, | 7 | *Two Women* | ⎫⎬ | Lent by George Campbell RHA |

## The Royal Institute of Oil Painters (ROI), London

| year | number | subject | price |
| --- | --- | --- | --- |
| 1932 | (Note: Conor the first Irishman to be elected an ROI) | | |
| | 115 | *Potato Gathering* | £ 15.15.0. |
| | 127 | *Point to Point* | £ 15.15.0. |
| | 209 | *An Ulster Fair* | £ 52.10.0. |
| | 256 | *Country Show – The Parade* (illustrated in catalogue) | £ 42. 0.0. |
| 1933 | 22 | *At The Fair* | £ 26. 5.5. |
| | 170 | *The Four Weavers* | £ 84. 0.0. |
| | 197 | *The Winner* (illustrated in catalogue) | £157. 0.0. |
| | 248 | *Cinerarias* | £ 26. 5.0. |
| 1934 | 157 | *Exercising Greyhounds* | £ 75. 0.0. |
| | 170 | *Start of the 25 yard race* (illustrated in catalogue) | £ 75. 0.0. |
| | 364 | *The Meet of the County Down Staghounds, Hills-borough* | £ 30. 0.0. |
| | 447 | *Coming From the Well* | £ 21. 0.0. |
| 1935 | 23 | *Curiosity* | £ 21. 0.0. |
| | 79 | *The Open-Air Market* | £ 42. 0.0. |
| | 222 | *The Cattle Auction* | £ 63. 0.0. |
| | 380 | *The Pony Fair* | £ 21. 0.0. |
| 1936 | 264 | *The Ship-workers* | £ 26. 5.0. |

|      | 277 | *The Fiddler* | £ 12.12.0. |
|------|-----|---------------|-----------|
|      | 363 | *Men of Iron* | £125. 0.0. |
|      | 443 | *The Third Generation* | £ 26. 5.0. |
| 1937 | 4 | *The Road to Glenties, Co Donegal* | £ 15.15.0. |
|      | 104 | *The Farmers' Race* | £ 75. 0.0. |
|      | 123 | *The Village Dance* | £ 21. 0.0. |
|      | 264 | *The Donkey-Cart* | £ 75. 0.0. |

## The Royal Society of Portrait Painters, London

| 1921 | oil | 170 | *R. V. Williams Esq.* (Richard Rowley) | |
|------|-----|-----|------|---|
| 1924 | ,, | 235 | *The Red-Haired Boy* | |
| 1928 | ,, | 109 | *The 'Gombeen Man'* | |
| 1930 | ,, | 95 | *Kitty* | |
|      | ,, | 134 | *The Musician* | |
| 1932 | ,, | 123 | *Elizabeth* | no prices |
|      | ,, | 205 | *A Namesake* (Conor's Mother) | |
| 1933 | ,, | 65 | *A Galway Blazer* | |
| 1934 | ,, | 84 | *Jean* | |
| 1935 | ,, | 226 | *My Brother* | |

## The Belfast Art Society/ Ulster Academy of Arts/ The Royal Ulster Academy

(The years marked * have titles taken from newspaper reviews as the catalogues cannot be located. Media mentioned where possible.)

| 1910 | w/c | 32 | *Reflections* | £ 2.10.0. |
|------|-----|-----|------|-----|
|      | w/c, etc | 251 | *Evening – Dufferin Dock* | £ 2. 2.0. |
|      | ,, ,, | 260 | *'Or Fantastic Bridge Athwart a Flood of Crystal'* | £ 3. 3.0. |
|      | ,, ,, | 270 | *Dredger, Milewater Basin* | £ 2. 2.0. |
|      | ,, ,, | 288 | *Unloading Coal, Albert Quay* | £ 2. 2.0. |
| 1911 | w/c | 15 | *The Hilly Road to Kinlough, Co Donegal* | £ 2. 2.0. |
|      | ,, | 237 | *Bundoran – East End* | £ 3. 3.0. |
|      | ,, | 263 | *Solitude* | £ 2. 2.0. |
| 1912 | w/c | 27 | *Ardara, Co Donegal* | £ 2. 2.0. |
|      | oil | 105 | *'The Curse'* | £ 3. 3.0. |
|      | w/c | 139 | *The Shady Pool* | £ 3. 3.0. |
|      | ,, | 190 | *The Windmill, Bangor, Co Down* | £ 2. 2.0. |
|      | ,, | 225 | *Running Water* | £ 3. 3.0. |
| 1913 | (Note: Conor elected on to the Committee of the Arts Society) | | | |
|      | w/c | 37 | *The Timber Ponds* | £ 3. 3.0. |
|      | ,, | 88 | *Ebb-tide* | £ 3. 3.0. |
|      | ,, | 129 | *Quay Side* | £ 3. 3.0. |
|      | oil | 157 | *The Lighterman* | £ 4. 4.0. |
|      | ,, | 253 | *A Woodland Stream* | £ 3. 3.0. |
| 1914 | — | 9 | *The Farm* | £ 2. 2.0. |
|      | oil | 65 | *The Half-Door* | £ 4. 4.0. |
|      | w/c | 92 | *Fight and Endure* | £ 3. 3.0. |

| | | | | | |
|---|---|---|---|---|---|
| | w/c | 97 | *War's Real Victim* | £ | 3. 3.0. |
| | oil | 205 | *The Recruit* | £ | 2. 2.0. |
| 1915 | w/c | 133 | *Bare Feet* | £ | 3. 3.0. |
| | pastel | 137 | *Languor* | £ | 3. 3.0. |
| | chalk | 215 | *Off! The Ulster Division* | £ | 3. 3.0. |
| 1916 | w/c | 41 | *The Accordion, Belfast St. Study* | £ | 5. 5.0. |
| | ,, | 74 | *Variety Market, Belfast* | £ | 2. 2.0. |
| | pastel | 119 | *The Milewater, Belfast* | £ | 3. 3.0. |
| | ,, | 121 | *The Patchwork Quilt* | £ | 21. 0.0. |
| | ,, | 130 | *Shades of Night* | £ | 3. 3.0. |
| 1917 | (Note: Conor elected for one year as one of the four Vice-Presidents) | | | | |
| | crayon | 1 | *Portrait Col. R. H. Wallace, C.B., D.L.* | ——— | |
| | ,, | 15 | *Portrait the late Lieut-Col. T. U. P. McCammon* | ——— | |
| | ,, | 41 | *Balloon Man* | £ | 10.10.0. |
| | ,, | 89 | *Portrait of Girl* | ——— | |
| | ,, | 126 | *Portrait of Little Girl* | ——— | |
| 1918 | w/c | 5 | *Elms* | £ | 10. 0.0. |
| | oil | 101 | *The Band Promenade, City Hall, Belfast* | £ | 40. 0.0. |
| | ,, | 193 | *The Weaver* | £ | 20. 0.0. |
| | crayon | 197 | *The Canadian* (portrait) | ——— | |
| 1919 | w/c | 39 | *Brenda* | ——— | |
| | ,, | 51 | *The Singers* | £ | 15.15.0. |
| | oil | 159 | *The Glorious Dead* | £100. 0.0. | |
| | ,, | 162 | *Chère Amie* | ——— | |
| | crayon | 245 | *Desmond Davey* | ——— | |
| 1920 | w/c | 16 | *Laughing Mill-girl* | £ | 12. 0.0. |
| | oil | 182 | *Miss Muriel Stewart* | ——— | |
| | ,, | 184 | *Summer: Noon* | £ | 15. 0.0. |
| | ,, | 185 | *Miss Carinna Davey* | ——— | |
| | ,, | 187 | *Fading Day* | £ | 10.10.0. |
| | ,, | 188 | *R. V. Williams, Esq.* | ——— | |
| 1921 | ,, | 157 | *The Twelfth* | £ | 60. 0.0. |
| | ,, | 169 | *Desmond* | £ | 60. 0.0. |
| | w/c | 95 | *The Street Preacher* | £ | 10. 0.0. |
| | ,, | 8 | *Half-timers* | £ | 5. 5.0. |
| 1922 | ,, | 17 | *Along at our Aise* | £ | 7. 7.0. |
| | oil | 196 | *The Melodeon Player* (lent by kind permission of Belfast Corporation) | ——— | |
| | ,, | 197 | *Portrait Study* | ——— | |
| | ,, | 202 | *Study for the painting of the Opening of the Northern Parliament* | £150. 0.0. | |
| | ,, | 211 | *The White Door* | £100. 0.0. | |
| | ,, | 247 | *Coortin* (lent by kind permission of Belfast Corporation) | ——— | |
| 1923 | w/c | 18 | *The Mote* | £ | 12.12.0. |
| | ,, | 45 | *Young Girl's Head* | £ | 10.10.0. |
| | ,, | 110 | *Street Preacher* | £ | 10.10.0. |
| | oil | 216 | *Sabbath Morning* | £ | 30. 0.0. |
| | ,, | 224 | *Bridal Morning* | £ | 80. 0.0. |
| | ,, | 230 | *Painter and Melodeon* | ——— | |
| 1924 | w/c | 8 | *Tantrums* | £ | 8. 8.0. |
| | ,, | 20 | *Mrs Walter Wheeler* | ——— | |
| | oil | 213 | *At the Door* | £ | 80. 0.0. |

| | | | | |
|---|---|---|---|---|
| | oil | 218 | *Miss Blanche Bennett (Mrs Edgar Adams)* | ——— |
| | ,, | 233 | *The Studio Dance* | ——— |
| | ,, | 265 | *The Pump* | £ 35. 0.0. |
| 1925 | w/c | 22 | *The Queen's Bridge, Belfast* | £ 10.10.0. |
| | ,, | 55 | *A. O. Meredith, Esq.* | ——— |
| | oil | 233 | *Francis A. Heron, Esq., D.L.* | ——— |
| | ,, | 234 | *Lynn Doyle, Esq.* | ——— |
| | ,, | 236 | *'1825'* | £ 52.10.0. |
| | ,, | 237 | *Eleanore* | ——— |

1926 (Note: Conor elected for one year as one of the four Vice-Presidents; no works shown as he was in America)

| | | | | |
|---|---|---|---|---|
| 1927 | oil | 8 | *The Crotal Coat* | ——— |
| | ,, | 12 | *The Marquess of Londonderry, K.G., Chancellor of Queen's University* | ——— |
| | ,, | 19 | *Mademoiselle Hagen* | ——— |
| | ,, | 26 | *Mrs. Alan McKibben* | ——— |
| | ,, | 55 | *The Old Cellist Player* | £ 30. 0.0. |
| | ,, | 64 | *6 o'clock* | £ 30. 0.0. |
| | w/c | 235 | *The Apprentice Boy* | n.f.s. |

1928 (Note: Conor elected for one year as one of the four Vice-Presidents)

| | | | | |
|---|---|---|---|---|
| | no | 54 | *The City Hall, Belfast* | £ 15.15.0. |
| | media | 70 | *The Art Student* | £100. 0.0. |
| | mentioned | 72 | *A Namesake* | ——— |
| | | 227 | *The Turf Gatherers* | £ 10.10.0. |
| | | 258 | *Master John Dawson Bates* | ——— |
| | | 311 | *A. C. Beaumont, Esq.* | ——— |
| 1929 | w/c | 161 | *On the Bridge* | £ 12.12.0. |
| | oil | 207 | *Mrs. Robert Marshall* | ——— |
| | ,, | 259 | *The Jaunting Car* | £100. 0.0. |
| | ,, | 263 | *Professor Andrew Fullerton, C.B., C.M.G.* | ——— |

*1930 (Note: Belfast Arts Society now called Ulster Academy of Arts. Conor, a founder member of the Academy, was elected one of the first nine Academicians)

| | | | | |
|---|---|---|---|---|
| | oil | 28 | *Saturday Night* | ——— |
| | ,, | 81 | *The Joke* (Self Portrait) | ——— |
| | ,, | 110 | *Alderman J. A. Doran* | ——— |
| 1931 | ,, | 55 | *Elizabeth* | ——— |
| | ,, | 74 | *Mrs. R. J. Smyllie* | ——— |
| | ,, | 79 | *The Polling Booth* | £130. 0.0. |

(No. 79 was the most highly priced in this exhibition)

| | | | | |
|---|---|---|---|---|
| *1932 | — | 66 | *On the Towpath* | ——— |
| | oil | 74 | *The Lord Chief Justice of Northern Ireland, Sir William Moore, K.C.* | ——— |
| | ,, | 82 | *The Painter's Mother* | ——— |

1933  
1934 } No pictures exhibited by Conor  
1935  
1936

1936 (On the 16th November Conor was elected an Honorary Academician)

| | | | | |
|---|---|---|---|---|
| 1937 1938 1939 1940 *1941 1942 *1943 | No pictures exhibited by Conor | | | |
| 1944 | oil | 30 | *The Sewing Machine Room* | £ 40. 0.0. |
| | ,, | 32 | *Waiting for the Excursion Train* | £130. 0.0. |
| | ,, | 46 | *Betty* | ——— |
| *1945 | ,, | | *It's One of Ours* | ——— |
| *1946 | ,, | No. 34 | *The Farmers' Race* | ——— |
| | — | 36 | *Miss Gladys Woods* | ——— |
| *1947 | ,, | | *Mrs Noel Johnston* | ——— |
| | ,, | | *Rev. Stewart Dickson* | ——— |
| | drawing | | *Miss Eileen Ayrton* | ——— |
| 1948 | oil | 33 | *Raymond* | ——— |
| | ,, | 53 | *The Path through the Woods* | £ 60. 0.0. |
| | w/c, etc. | 234 | *Dorothy Parke* | ——— |
| 1949 | oil | 41 | *Corinne in Furs* | ——— |
| | ,, | 44 | *Listening to the Band* | £120. 0.0. |
| | w/c, etc. | 220 | *A Cup of Tay* | £ 18.18.0. |

1950 (Note: the Ulster Academy of Arts now called The Royal Ulster Academy of Art)

| | | | | |
|---|---|---|---|---|
| | oil | 62 | *Going to the Races* | £ 60. 0.0. |
| | ,, | 106 | *Robert Lynd* | ——— |
| | w/c, etc. | 219 | *The Restive Cart-Horse* | £ 21. 0.0. |
| 1951 | oil | 33 | *Launching a Cruiser* | £150. 0.0. |
| | w/c, etc. | 159 | *Fife and Drums* | £ 25. 0.0. |
| | ,, ,, | 176 | *Lunch-hour in the City Hall Grounds* | £ 23. 0.0. |
| 1952 | oil | 57 | *Cantering to the Starting Gate* | £ 65. 0.0. |
| | w/c, etc. | 183 | *When Day is Done* | £ 25. 0.0. |
| | ,, ,, | 187 | *Motherhood* | £ 25. 0.0. |
| 1953 | oil | 51 | *Open Air Market* | £ 60. 0.0. |
| | w/c, etc. | 192 | *Joe Kennedy's Ferry Boat* | £ 25. 0.0. |
| | ,, ,, | 208 | *The Sulky Child* | £ 24. 0.0. |
| 1954 | oil | 30 | *Captain J. W. Storey, O.B.E., B.A.* | ——— |
| | ,, | 31 | *Fred Story Esq., C.B.E.* | ——— |
| | w/c, etc. | 142 | *Rosy Apples* | £ 25. 0.0. |
| 1955 | oil | 34 | *Portrait of an Artist* (self portrait) | ——— |
| | w/c, etc. | 144 | *The Sash My Father Wore* | £ 30. 0.0. |
| | ,, ,, | 150 | *The Woman Next Door* | £ 23. 0.0. |
| 1956 | oil | 31 | *The Jockey* | £ 56. 0.0. |
| | ,, | 74 | *Here Comes the Bride* | £150. 0.0. |
| | w/c, etc. | 144 | *With a Smile and a Song* | £ 30. 0.0. |

1957 (Note: Conor elected President of the R.U.A.)

| | | | | |
|---|---|---|---|---|
| | oil | 18 | *Fun of the Fair* | £125. 0.0. |
| | w/c | 108 | *Sally* | £ 31.10.0. |
| | ,, | 133 | *Coal Buckets* | ——— |

Media sections no longer mentioned in the catalogues

1958 R.U.A. Spring Exhibition

| | | | |
|---|---|---|---|
| | 26 | *Along the Lagan* | £ 42. 0.0. |
| | 88 | *Over they go* | £ 26. 5.0. |
| 1958 | 12 | *The Sleeping Cat* | £ 31.10.0. |

|      |     |                                   |              |
|------|-----|-----------------------------------|--------------|
|      | 13  | *The Shipyard Worker*             | £ 21. 0.0.   |
|      | 28  | *The Story-Teller*                | £150. 0.0.   |
| 1959 | 98  | *Country Polling Booth*           | £147. 0.0.   |
|      | 99  | *Wednesday's Child*               | £105. 0.0.   |
|      | 100 | *Between the Dances*              | £ 26. 5.0.   |
| 1960 | 7   | *Forever and Ever*                | £ 84. 0.0.   |
|      | 28  | *The Child Next Door*             | £ 52.10.0.   |

1961 R.U.A. Spring Exhibition

|      |     |                                   |              |
|------|-----|-----------------------------------|--------------|
|      | 13  | *The Odd Child*                   | n.f.s.       |
| 1961 | 19  | *Hitting the Flure*               | £ 31.10.0.   |
|      | 20  | *I Saw a Maiden*                  | £ 52.10.0.   |
|      | 21  | *Lambegs*                         | £ 35.15.0.   |
| 1962 | 56  | *What is in the News?*            | ————         |
|      | 57  | *Long Ago Days*                   | £110. 0.0.   |
|      | 79  | *The Heavy Child*                 | £ 52. 0.0.   |
| 1963 | 49  | *A Far Out Friend*                | £120. 0.0.   |
|      | 53  | *'All Alone am I'*                | £120. 0.0.   |
|      | 72  | *Those Were the Days*             | £ 30. 0.0.   |

1964 (Note: Conor's last year as President before retirement)

|      |     |                                          |              |
|------|-----|------------------------------------------|--------------|
|      | 11  | *Over and Away*                          | £ 25. 0.0.   |
|      | 52  | *Songs of Praise*                        | £120. 0.0.   |
|      | 60  | *Long time Ago*                          | £ 25. 0.0.   |
| 1965 | 58  | *The Belfast Opera House at Night, 1906* | £115.10.0.   |
|      | 59  | *Queueing in the Rain*                   | £115.10.0.   |
|      | 60  | *The Twelfth*                            | £ 27. 6.0.   |

When this exhibition went to Londonderry, Catalogue No. 60 changed to:

|      |     |                                   |              |
|------|-----|-----------------------------------|--------------|
|      | 60  | *When Day is Done*                | £ 26. 5.0.   |
| 1966 | 6   | *Lambegs*                         | £150. 0.0.   |
|      | 7   | *Sweet and Twenty*                | £ 20. 0.0.   |
|      | 8   | *By the Cool Waters*              | £ 20. 0.0.   |
| 1967 | 5   | *Belfast Strike*                  | £105. 0.0.   |
|      | 6   | *Balloon Man*                     | £ 26. 0.0.   |
|      | 7   | *Dutchie*                         | £ 20. 0.0.   |

1968 5th February death of William Conor

The Academy included a Memorial Show of 7 Conor pictures:

|      |     |                                                            |         |
|------|-----|------------------------------------------------------------|---------|
|      | 4   | *Approaching the Starting Gate* (Diploma Work) (Coll. R.U.A.) | n.f.s.  |
|      | 5   | *George Galway MacCann as a Young Man* (Coll. Mrs. Mercy MacCann) | n.f.s.  |
|      | 6   | *Rest and be Thankful* (Coll. Mr. Harry Cooke Knox)        | n.f.s.  |
|      | 7   | *Portrait of a Young Girl 1924* (Coll. Miss M. Y. Lawrence) | n.f.s.  |
|      | 8   | *The Child Next Door* (Coll. Miss M. Y. Lawrence)          | n.f.s.  |
|      | 9   | *St. George's Market, Belfast, 1909* (Coll. Miss M. Y. Lawrence) | n.f.s.  |
|      | 10  | *Barges by the Lagan* (Coll. Miss M. Y. Lawrence)          | n.f.s.  |